Immigrants
Vol I

Capital of Immigrants

Shimon Garber

© 2017 Shimon Garber

Editor, Russian text: Anastasia Olshevskya
Corrector, Russian version: Ludmilla Shilina
Translated: By Shimon Garber
Design: Michael Grossman

Authors Newcomers Publishing Group
ISBN-13: 978-1-950430383; HC
ISBN-13: 978-1-950430390; Epub

Fourth edition 2022
LCCN: TX 8-222-174
2023

Contents

Preface 1

It's Only the Beginning 3

Childhood Dreams
and Adult Desires 11

Migrants' Vienna 16

Vienna; HIAS 26

Vienna—Night Fears 31

Damen Von Madam 40

Zum Turken 54

Diana-Bad 60

New Year's Eve
in Vienna 65

Meetings in Vienna 73

Arrival in New York 92

The First Apartment 99

English Language
Courses 105

Roma Di Notte 121

Orsini's 130

Dinner at Orsini's 141

Chicken Kiev 150

Penne ala Vodka 159

Celebrities at Orsini's 168

Meetings in New York 174

San Diego 181

Forest Hills 186

Companions 196

Sizzler Restaurant 201

Montreal 208

The First Business 225

Cookbook 231

Christmas Baby 236

Time for Change 245

Partners 253

Limousine Service 263

Ask Limousine 274

Atlantic City 283

Dear reader–

This book is a translation from an original manuscript written in Russian, and like any translation, it only partially captures the spirit of the original. However, it might still offer a glimpse into what life was like for an immigrant during the last decades of the twentieth century.

The author

Preface

THE PROTAGONIST IS ADAM GARDOV, a Soviet citizen of Jewish origin who, in the 1970s, was able to emigrate from the Soviet Union. After leaving Russia, he flew to Austria, where representatives of the Israeli agency Sohnut greeted him and changed plans. He decides, instead of Israel, to continue to the United States. Waiting for an American visa takes six months; during that time, Adam works in Vienna for one of the more odious characters involved in immigration during those years—Madame Betina.

During his six months in Vienna, Adam meets with various people, characters, and destinies. In Austria, he becomes acquainted with his future wife, Nata. He will later send her through the Italian route for immigrants, where she waits for permission to enter America.

Madame Betina (as everyone called her) offers to assist in obtaining an Austrian residence permit, but Adam refuses to accept it. And when he receives his US visa, he does not hesitate to depart to New York—the city of his dreams.

Life in New York presents challenges that are rarely pleasant for foreigners: learning an unfamiliar language, finding an apartment, and finding a job. Quite typically, for many immigrants, a series of changing occupations end with the intent to start a small business. Adam tries to establish a business with former compatriots, but as Russians often say, *"the first pancake always does not go so well."* It was a failure, and the second attempt was no better. But Adam does not surrender, and while working as a waiter, cashier, and bartender, he cherishes his dream of having his own business in the restaurant sector.

On the bright side are an unexpected second encounter with Nata and the realization that she is his love—his fate is to have a family. They get married and have a daughter.

The story of Adam partly repeats the tortuous journey of other immigrants who have moved from their temporary residence in Europe to the United States. Adaptation, the ups, the downs, family. New hopes. Another attempt to open a new business and a determination to get his place on American soil. However, unlike many, Adam tried not to depend on the grace of fate and worked hard to achieve his dream.

It's Only the Beginning

HE LEFT EVERYTHING BEHIND: his past life, work, friends, and the country where he was born and raised. Ahead lay a different culture, an unfamiliar language, and an alien world.

The grown man, Adam, sat in an airplane, considering the porthole in the clouds that hid his misty future. He felt a childish fear of something new, unknown. No one nearby would say the words to calm him down.

"Don't be afraid; everything will be fine."

Mother had died a long time ago, and although Adam was active, having grown up in USSR on the harsh streets of Leningrad, he now would give anything to hear his mom's encouraging words—or just her voice—calling him. Despite the desire to leave the old country and go anywhere to start living a new life, memories had always been with him from childhood.

* * *

Adam, as a young boy, ran to a particular store to buy kerosene for the little stove needed to cook in the kitchen. He clutched the tin can handle when he heard the loudspeakers, suspended like

dead crows hanging on the walls of the houses. The announcer told the terrible, impossible news in a loud voice.
"*Death of the greatest world leader, Joseph Stalin!*"
People were frozen in shock. Many wept, not hesitating to show their tears. They repeated aloud the same questions to each other. "How are we without him? How are we going to live now?"
How can I live now?
Adam also cried deeply in sorrow. He had heard about the danger, the country surrounded by too many enemies, and Comrade Stalin knew all of this and could defend Russia. Adam still couldn't believe it.
Now he has died. Consequently, we all will perish.
Adam's fear was great. He had never known his father's love and care, and the loss of the leader who had personified the image of a father made Adam terrified.
Rumors of the cause of the leader's death were heard everywhere. But amazingly enough, the world had not crashed, and life continued.
People went to work and had meals, maybe without their previous joy, but still found some pleasure.
One of the boys stood up in the classroom. He was crying and angry. "They were Jews—the doctors who killed Comrade Stalin!"
The teacher explained that this was wrong and that Comrade Stalin had died from severe disease. But many didn't believe that. Adam was just a boy and did not see how he was guilty or responsible for the tragedy of the Soviet people, but he had heard gossip about the Jewish race's responsibility. He had to get used to hiding his feelings.

Once in the classroom, the children argued, "Is Adam a Jew?" One of his friends and fellow students claimed, "Adam is Russian because, despite the suspicious name, his surname, Gardov, ends with 'ov.' As we all know, all Russian surnames end with 'ov' or 'in.'"

Everyone checked their names against these proposed endings and agreed to be true.

Adam would shrug. *"I should ask Mom,"* responding to a direct question.

He knew the response in advance. His wise, loving mom always taught him, "If anyone asks, just say that your deceased father was Russian."

Other rumors went around that Comrade Stalin was not such a good man. Talking or even thinking about this was scary. Adam read a lot and had his own opinion; doubt sharpened his youthful curiosity.

Something strange was happening in the country. Comrade Beria, Stalin's ally and friend, seemed now an enemy and a spy. Then, during a power struggle, one leader after another ruled the country, but they all died one after another pretty soon.

But as one of the leaders (Gorbachev) said, the "process had started."

Freedom-loving people were given prison sentences or were placed in mental institutions. Some people spread handwritten books among the population. The books were called "self-publishing," and they said awful things about Comrade Stalin and the repression of dissenters.

Whispers of disapproval among free-thinking people grew louder; people feared no more and made jokes about the hilariously drawn revolution world and even the Communist Party.

If everything was a lie, and Stalin was a bad person, higher Communist Party authorities are either fools or lackeys and hangers-on; how will we live from now on in this country? Now all must be changed. The ulcer has been revealed. All masks are taken off, and we will continue now that the wound is clean and can heal, and the people will live freely and joyfully.

* * *

Alas, this did not happen. Adam grew up and waited for changes to come. The 1970s was a period of stagnation, branded in the years to come. One leader replaced the other deceased party chairman and then came one more leader, but nothing changed. All those same sycophantic faces flickered on TV; it made Adam sick even to look at the triumph of stupidities.

When climbing the career ladder, Adam used to tell his friends, "I'll wait until I reach thirty years old, and then, somehow, I'll leave from here. I do not want to spend my life in combat with foolishness and lies."

The situation in Russia was getting worse and worse. People became poorer; goods became more expensive. People in the queues for food resented that bread was mixed with peas and that whale fat was added to the butter. Many foodstuffs, as well as other products, disappeared from retail stores. The USSR, an exporter of wheat, transformed into an importer. It was necessary to purchase vast quantities of grain to feed the whole hungry country. Then the Americans pushed through the Jackson-Vanik

Amendment to the Trade Act 1974. That Trade Act made the sale of vast quantities of grain to Russia dependent on freedom for Russian Jews, allowing them to leave for Israel.

L. Brezhnev, at that time the leader of the Communist Party of Russia, was believed to have been on drugs in his later years of rule. He had decided that for the Soviet people, there was no remaining choice.

The country needed grain badly, and some Jews could go in exchange for permission to buy grain at a fair price from the United States; Russia allowed Jews to reunite with relatives living in Israel. It gave rise to envy and resentment, and many mixed marriages were created in which one of the parties was an offshoot of the Jewish nationality.

The flow of emigration had grown, expanding increasingly, and it threatened to carry out half of the country.

Despite this new policy, the KGB believed that emigrants were holders of classified information and could give secrets to enemies of the Soviet motherland. However, many people couldn't leave the country. How all the marriages occurred was the secret of the honeymooners, but subsequent divorces spoke for themselves.

The leaders shut off the valve because of the danger of losing many of the country's specialists and scientists.

People applying for permission to leave took severe risks. Many who were denied permission to leave were branded with so-called "black labels" for the rest of their lives and could only work as street or chimney cleaners. Those hoping to leave were going through public condemnation by colleagues and were excluded from society. The desire to leave the USSR was considered a rebellion against the system. The country was full of citizens infected with a "virus of freedom."

Emigrants could not take any documents: passports, birth certificates, diplomas, or state awards. They became disenfranchised. Obtaining an exit permit depended on one's ability to repay for receiving higher education. For many, this became a serious obstacle. Among those wishing to leave were many intelligent and educated people. In addition, emigrants had to give up their Soviet citizenship at the cost of five hundred rubles. It was a large amount of money for those times. Understandably, apartments and other wealth could not be sold. It was prohibited. For those wishing to sell personal belongings, there were special pawn shops. If someone had something valuable, they would place it there and wait until it sold. There would be some commission for the store, of course.

People were given forms that detailed lists of people and organizations they had to sign for final authorization, and then they obtained permission to leave. Authorities later realized the problem with the immigrant flow; in the 1980s, the stream closed.

* * *

Adam was lucky; he decided to apply in late 1978. He worked at state *dachas* (reception places for important state guests during their stay in the country), and, unsurprisingly, this work could suddenly be classified. Was he afraid of some background check issue? Of course, the carriers of such information may not leave the country because they could transmit it.

In addition, in 1978, Adam's sister, Sonya, left the USSR with her young son. This detail did not escape the attention of the regulatory authorities. The head of the administration where Adam worked was informed. Their relationship was friendly, respectful, and supported financially. Adam could be the cause of many problems for his boss.

"Listen, Adam, you know I always respect you. Therefore, I will not beat around the bush. It was leaked from the top that your sister went to Israel. I guess you are also going? No, do not say anything. You're the director of our central city enterprise. It is an issue for many people. I'll transfer you into the outlying district of Kupchino so that for both of us, it will be calmer."

Adam soon got an invitation from "Israel's relatives" and resigned voluntarily. He read a sad regret on his boss's face. Still, he seemed relieved when he signed Adam's dismissal and passed to his hands a particular document called an employment book—an essential document needed for registration at any job in Russia. Both understood that only through timely handling had Adam managed to avoid a layoff with the stigma of the traitor, which would mean big trouble for his superiors. The next stage of preparing for departure was filling out a document package at OVIR, the division dealing with visas and registrations. Adam hoped to be lucky. In case of refusal, he could fight and repeatedly apply but with well-known prospects of success. If refused, he would have to start afresh, search for accommodations, and find a job, which meant a miserable life.

For two months, Adam waited in fear and anticipation. When the call came from OVIR, he was shaking. He tried to guess who he would be in a couple of hours: a free man or an outcast. Fate favored him; OVIR gave the go-ahead.

But another problem loomed: the letter issued required the signature of his former wife, with an obligatory indication of the absence of any substantive claims.

Two years back, he had married; he did not quite understand why he married this woman. The three-bedroom apartment they had bought went to his wife in exchange for signing the so-called "certificate of absence of material and other claims."

The relationship, in reality, did not work out, and the divorce had to go through court. Adam got out of the marriage, owned a car, rejoiced that all the problems with property were solved.

His former spouse would have to sign yet another form, but surprisingly, everything went smoothly. This form was signed, and Adam went to the bank. He had to pay a fee of five hundred rubles to renounce his citizenship. He could exchange currency with an OVIR particular letter and get $150, the maximum any emigrant could take out.

Adam sat on a plane leaving for Vienna, Europe's most beautiful city. It was the distribution point for *renegades* and *traitors* of the Soviet motherland. With this sum and without documentation, he had no idea what the future would bring.

Childhood Dreams and Adult Desires

ADAM GREW UP IN LENINGRAD, the former Saint Petersburg, after the siege of World War II. For entertainment, the children played volleyball. On dark evenings, games were off, and guys sat on logs in the courtyard, smoking stolen cigarettes. With such a meager selection of activities, it was unsurprising that Adam became addicted to reading and spent more time with books than with other boys.

Adam signed up for the three public libraries and could get six books at a time. Each library doled out only two books simultaneously: one could be fiction, and the other had to be scientific. He read while sitting, lying, and standing; he read everywhere he could open a book—at the table, standing in line, or lying on the bed or floor. He would read day or night, anywhere he could. The books took him into another world, unlike where he lived. He found freedom to travel in that world, a triumph of bold ideas, common sense, and earned-wealth stories. He dreamed that someday he would be in that world. And he was stubborn and sure that he would do anything necessary to make such a dream come true. He told his friends that he wanted to visit there someday.

* * *

Adam left for New York—in the literal sense, thanks to the books. Why he was not put in some school for difficult children was a mystery. Perhaps such talk wasn't punished; probably no one took it seriously; too much reading, stupid childish behavior. But life could be strange.

By the end of the seventies, still in Leningrad, Adam was hospitalized due to stomach problems. And there, he met a man who attracted his attention because he was reading a book in English. Adam came over and asked softly, "Leaving?"

"How could you tell?"

Adam pointed at the book and looked straight into the eyes of the stranger. It immediately became clear that both wanted to go—or, at least, desperately wanted to try.

Igor turned out to be a teacher of medical science. He was a pleasant man who was easy to talk to. They exchanged phone numbers and eventually became firm friends.

They visited each other for drinks and chats, dreaming about life in New York.

Igor was married to Margaret, who everyone called simply beautiful Margo. She had some Italian blood and a bright appearance that unwittingly arrested attention. They had a nine-year-old son; he and his mother were like two peas in a pod.

Capital of Immigrants

Igor and his family migrated first, and two months behind them, Adam followed.

Somehow, on the day before Adam's departure, Igor called "from over there" and said, "Before you get to Vienna, you will have a stop at Budapest. Spend your $150 on cigarettes; here, you can sell them for a fair price. Take a jar of caviar, a bottle of Soviet champagne, and a bottle of vodka."

Adam did so.

* * *

The plane landed in Vienna. All Jewish migrants from the Soviet Union were always greeted by Sohnut, representing Israel's Ministry of Absorption.

Stray thoughts flashed in Adam's head. *Maybe I should not go to America? Maybe I should go to Israel, the historic birthplace of the Jewish nation. Yes or no? But we decided with Igor to conquer New York together. He is my only friend in this new life. Such friendship is not easy to find.*

Austrian customs were very simple: they took away the cigarettes. Meeting migrants, the Israeli representatives spoke Russian and had typical Soviet hospitality.

"Going to America? Go to the left. If you are going to Israel, move to the right."

There was no hello or goodbye. After such a "warm reception," Adam did not doubt where to migrate.

Enough of this socialist rudeness for me. I am going to America.

Future USA citizens were put on a bus and taken to Vienna. Everything happened quickly, and Adam fell into a daze.

Where have they taken us? What can happen to us?
The migrants did not know the answers to these questions. It was simply scary. The bus stopped at a small building, and the newly arrived migrants were dropped off. The building resembled a small hotel. A crowd of migrants was welcomed by a petite but very energetic lady who spoke Russian with an eerie emphasis.

"My name is Madam Betina. You are at the Hotel *Zum Turken.* Congratulations on arriving in a free world! My assistants, Ilya and Igor, will tell you everything."

She quickly disappeared, and Adam was pleasantly surprised to recognize one of the assistants—his comrade Igor. He warmly greeted Adam and took him into the adjacent room.

"Stay in here while we deal with everything. Then we'll go to my house. Today you'll have to sleep there."

Adam thanked fate for sending him this meeting. They took a taxi in the evening and went to Igor's home.

The apartment was significant; it had two bedrooms and chic furnishings. Igor's wife, Margo, and their son, Bennie, met Adam as a long-awaited guest.

"It seems that housing is not cheap," Adam could not help mentioning.

"Yes, but it is paid for by the organization we are members of. However, we will talk about such affairs later. For now, we should celebrate your arrival and freedom."

Margo always prepared tasty meals, and Adam, who knew much about good food, paid tribute to her talent. Of course, during the dinner, the conversation was about their abandoned homeland, a temporary refuge in Vienna, and—most importantly—the future in America. Igor and Margo used to work as dentists in Russia and hoped to pass the qualifying exam to help them find early employment in the USA. His American colleagues often visited the USSR for international seminars and predicted that Igor would have a future in the United States. Igor had been preparing for the departure for a long time, knew some dentists in New York, and counted on their help and advice.

"And you, Adam, did you not change your mind? Do you still want to open a restaurant in New York?"

"I did not change my mind. I know this business inside out, and I want to do it. My problem is seed capital."

"You know that American dentists earn a good bunch of money?"

"Of course. And I hope that you're also going to do as well."

"It's not a question of how to earn money but how to save and multiply money. I will invest money in your restaurant, and we both can get rich. Is this a good plan?"

"Great plan! I couldn't have dreamed of a better companion. You can be sure your investment will pay off with a profit."

"Businessmen, it seems time to retire," Margo laughed. "Tomorrow, we will share the profits. Adam, let's go; I shall put you in the guest room."

That night in Vienna, the capital of Austria, Adam fell asleep as a free man with a smile on his lips and a million ideas in his head. It seemed that everything had finally become simple, direct, and possible.

Migrants' Vienna

VIENNA HAD BECOME A TRANSIT POINT for all migrants from Russia. When Adam stayed in Viena that year, a record number of migrants from the USSR passed through—fifty-nine thousand people. Most went to Israel and America, and a few went to Germany and South Africa. Groups heading to Israel right out of the airport were taken to an old Austrian castle, where they waited for a few days for the first available plane. Shooters guarded these migrants; the government feared terrorists. The remaining migrants stayed in Vienna for a week and then were on trains to Italy. In the suburbs of Rome—Ostia and Ladispoli—they lived for about six months in anticipation of American visas. Migrants were supported by the charity HIAS, which originated in 1881, assumed monetary expenditures, and did not distinguish between Jewish and non-Jewish people. HIAS assisted with small cash benefits for migrants until they solved their organizational and bureaucratic issues.

People from Moscow and Saint Petersburg arrived in Vienna by plane, and the rest, from all over Russia, came by train, to the delight of customs. The Russian customs officials searched people at the border, and everything of value was taken.

A particularly awful practice prevailed at the last station, called "Chop." This border point between the Soviet Union and Hungary was the last place the border guards could search for luggage. Belongings were thrown from wagons; suitcases were smashed on the ground, searching for anything valuable. Arguing was useless. At Leningrad's airport, customs had another peculiarity: "traitors" to the homeland were stripped naked and searched in the most intimate places. Lawlessness and covetousness concerning "traitors leaving the motherland" had been sanctioned from above. In Vienna, the representative of HIAS was Madam Betina, as everyone called her, a frail but incredibly energetic woman. She and her husband owned two hotels: Zum Turken and Danau. Every day, 200 to 250 new migrants from Russia arrived in Vienna. Madam Betina gave temporary shelter to exhausted, terrified, desperate people. Her job was to receive and check in new arrivals.

She gave them cash for the first three days (three dollars a day per person), and, most importantly, provided shelter to settle. Many families had infants or helpless, elderly relatives with disabilities. The Spartan surroundings of the two hotels were reminiscent of army barracks.

"My God! They're so old and sick. Why were they tormented and dragged here?" cried Madam Betina.

"But what can we do? Leave them over there, in Russia? What would they say then?"

Madam Betina had a contract with HIAS to settle any number of migrants. But nobody anticipated that there would be so many. For every migrant who got to Vienna and went through her service, Madam Betina received a certain amount from HIAS, and business had been very profitable.

But the wave of people kept flooding. It seemed that Vienna would drown from the flow of migrants. Madam Betina spent days searching through the city for available places, ready to pay any money for housing exhausted migrants. She rented hotels and private apartments—anything that could shelter boatloads of people.

Hotel Zum Turken was the headquarters, housing migrants from airports and train stations. From the hotel, taxis transported them around town. Families were looking for housing that had kitchens. Single people were sent to hotels, and two to four people were placed in each room.

Madam Betina employed two people who were the solution to all the problems of migrants: Igor and Ilya. Adam assessed the scale and severity of their work only later. Igor's new talents stunned him, and Adam listened to what he was saying.

"Firstly, you need someplace to stay. The Zum Turken has a general kitchen; you can cook some meals, but each room can hold four or even ten people. Moreover, it is far from the center. Betina has another hotel called Danau; it's close to my house. Of course, it is not the Hilton, but there are double rooms and a kettle with boiling water for tea. The big apartments are for families with children, only in Danau. We call it Dachau. Do not be frightened. Tomorrow you'll go with Margo to HIAS. Register, get money for a week, and that's all. Then you'll wait for transport to Italy."

"And why didn't you leave for Italy?" Wondered Adam.

"I was recommended to work with Madam Betina, and Margo and I decided to process migration in Vienna."

"So, maybe I also can stay here?"

"It's not that easy. HIAS does not pay for migration in Vienna. We moved on to another Jewish organization called Rav Tov."

"Can I do the same?"

"Probably, yes. Are you sure you do not want to go to Italy?"

Adam didn't want to go.

"Okay," Igor replied, "let's go to Danau and check whether rooms are available. Later on, I'll take you to Rav Tov."

Igor arranged a residence for Adam, and they returned to Zum Turken for Adam's suitcase. Danau was a two-story structure with numerous rooms crammed full of migrants from Russia. In the corridors, kids ran and buzzed aloud.

"Igor, you ride all the time in taxis. It's quite expensive."

"The company pays. I give my receipts to Madam Betina, and that's it."

"And she is not aware?"

"No, she knows everything. Every day we send ten to fifteen cars with migrants to living places. One or two more taxis do not make any difference."

The taxi stopped at the Zum Turken.

"Adam, that's what we will do now. I'll talk with Ilya, and if I don't have anything to do right now, we can go to the Rav Tov. Then go back to Danau and unpack your suitcases. You have some free time. I'll be in the lobby."

Adam nodded and went wandering through Zum Turken. This place had become well-known among migrants. In big rooms stood bunk beds. Doors were wide open, and people scurried back and forth. In a big kitchen, women cooked food on a large stove. The broth smelled of cheap chicken gizzards.

Women stirring soups reminisced, "These chicken gizzards were considered a great delicacy at home. And now our ungrateful husbands gripe that this is the same thing every day for dinner."

The vast, communal apartment reminded Adam that his childhood home had been the home of many families; they prepared meals together in an enclosure of a few square meters. Each woman cooked for her own family. Some washed clothes simultaneously and gossiped about their husbands and neighbors. It was simple; this was migration.

"Adam, are you here?" Igor appeared in the doorway. "Oh, yes, the kitchen is your weakness. We will go to the Rav Tov now. I called them. They're waiting for us."

Shortly they went into the small office of some religious organization. A middle-aged man in a black suit and a black hat spoke English with a friendly smile and a willingness to help. He congratulated Adam on his arrival into the free world. Igor translated. Adam understood little about what was happening, but Igor had already gone through all this. Adam could only trust Igor's experience and did not ask any questions. When they said goodbye to the rabbi of Rav Tov, Igor concluded, "In short, everything is fine. They need documents from HIAS, and everything else they will do themselves."

"Igor, thank you so much. I don't even know how to thank you for everything. I have no money now, you know. And my cigarettes were seized at the border."

"Of course. I completely forgot!" Igor slapped himself on the forehead. "We need to pick them up today."

"What do you mean, pick them up?"

Capital of Immigrants

"They are in the customs warehouse. We have a man who'll come to Zum Turken. I'm going to call him."

To say that the new talent of his friend struck Adam was an understatement. Madam Betina was waiting for them in the hotel; she was angry. "Igor, where did you go? People are coming from the airport. The hotel is already so full of people, Ilya, and I no longer know how to accommodate everyone."

Adam did not know when Igor would be available again; the reception of the immigrants could drag on until night. Adam considered the best way to avoid the confusion and followed the advice of his friend; he went to take a nap in Ilya's room. Ilya's stuff was scattered on the bottom shelf of the bunk bed. Adam decided to climb up on the bed above. But as he threw off a blanket, he froze, startled.

On the mattress lay rows of bottles of vodka and champagne, jars with black caviar, souvenirs, and chains with beads of unfamiliar material. All this, no doubt, was brought from Russia. Adam quickly covered these riches with a blanket and looked around. No, no one had followed him or seen him.

Whose is this? Ilya's? Adam thought. *But how did he bring it? No, it's unreal. And what can he do with this? Why the devil is there so much food and alcohol? Oh, this is what he bought, probably. Migrants who have arrived brought this. Then it could be sold to someone, but to whom? It's generally not my business. I brought with me the same set of things. It was not confiscated at customs. I can give it to Igor as a thank-you for his help.*

Igor appeared an hour later, holding a few bottles of vodka and champagne. "Adam, take off the blanket." He put all the stuff on the mattress. "Don't cover it. I'll bring some more."

He left and quickly returned, carrying jars of black caviar and more bottles. He exhaled with the last lot. "Uff, that's it. All done. Now let's deal with your problem."

"Igor, I also have caviar, vodka, and champagne in the bag," mentioned Adam.

"Why are you so silent? Take it out. So, a jar of caviar is one hundred and thirty schillings, vodka is forty, and champagne is thirty. The total is two hundred schillings. Here it is."

"Igor! You do not understand. That is for you. It's a gift."

"Don't talk nonsense. This money is yours. Who do you take me for?"

Igor dismissively shoved crisp money at Adam and changed the subject.

"Now, we'll take care of the problem with your cigarettes." He dialed a number. "Hello, Mark? Hey, this is Igor from Zum Turken. Remember that I talked about my friend with cigarettes? Yes, four blocks of Marlboros. When? Tonight? Can you pick him up at Danau? It's cool."

Igor hung up and smiled. "Mark will come for you at ten thirty tonight. He will get the cigarettes from the warehouse, and you will sell them to him at a discount. Okay?"

"Of course, it's okay. Thank you, Igor."

"Let's go; I will drop you at Danau."

* * *

Capital of Immigrants

Adam had to share a room at Danau with a neighbor. He was cheerful, clearly under the influence of alcohol.

"My friend … here is pure alcohol, sold in pharmacies for forty schillings. Good, pure, and we can drink it. Can you imagine? Want to drink?"

"No, thanks. I've got something to do."

"Well, as you wish. I'll drink a little."

Adam slid his gaze to his neighbor and realized that "a little" had already been exceeded. There was some time remaining before Adam would meet Mark. He felt hungry and decided to take a stroll and buy some food. He walked around the city, astonished at the beautiful streets, clean sidewalks, and numerous cafés. Well-dressed people hurried about their business without worrying about migrants' problems, destinies, and issues. It was entirely someone else's life and seemingly carefree. Adam felt very sorry for himself.

They danced the waltz under the sound of Strauss while we struggled over there. Would they try waltzing in postwar Leningrad when all struggled for a piece of bread? Oh, why does it bother me? It's time to learn to be as they are—without worries. Have to forget about the Soviet gloominess, concerns, and judgments. Indeed, they have enough own problems.

He passed by a café where, through an open window, he saw golden, slightly browned whole chickens on a grill. They smelled delicious, and his stomach growled from hunger. *When was the last time I had eaten?*

A signboard read, *"Just 28 shillings!"*

Interesting, how much is it? Is it per piece, serving, or kilogram?

Adam handed the vendor a hundred-schilling bill and got a plastic fork, knife, and a hot, whole chicken on a paper plate. He counted the change and understood he could afford this chicken with his daily subsistence minimum. He sat down on the street at the table and gobbled, counting the change, trying to transfer schillings into dollars and dollars into rubles.

Not bad. If I had it for daily lunch, I would not be hungry, even at the allowance limit. I could eat the same chicken every day, as some other people do. It's going to be all right. My daily life here is established.

Adam wrapped an unfinished chicken leg in a napkin and slowly returned to the Danau. He did not want to meet his roommate and refused an offer to drink a little bit, so he waited for Mark at the hotel entrance.

A car pulled up at the appointed time, and a young fellow in the car called to him. "You Adam? Hi, let's go."

Mark raced toward the railroad station. When they arrived on the scene, it was already dark. They waited for a man in the uniform of a railroad employee. He came, and they had a brief conversation in German. Then everyone strode along the tracks with wagons, following the shining light of a flashlight onto the road. Adam and Mark barely kept up with this guard. The sky was moonless and dark. Finally, a faint flashlight beam illuminated the dark side of one of the goods wagons.

"Here!" announced a railwayman. He pushed the door back with a loud sound and disappeared into the depths of the car. After a few minutes, he popped up out of the darkness of the wagon and handed Adam a parcel.

"Yours?"

He peeked into the package; there were four blocks of Marlboro cigarettes.

"Yes, it's mine."

Marlboros were Marlboros. What was the difference?

Adam wasn't sure it was his; he didn't put the labels on the cigarettes. How would he distinguish whose they were?

Mark chatted softly about something with the railway worker, who melted into the night. Adam gave Mark the cigarettes in the car and received the money. They parted ways at the door of the Danau, very pleased with the transaction.

Vienna; HIAS

MARGO CAME INTO THE DANAU EARLY to accompany Adam into the *HIAS*. Her appearance stirred up all the males, and Adam's roommate could not resist eyeing their guest.

He snorted, "You are so lucky, my friend! You didn't say that you had such a gorgeous girlfriend."

"She's not my girlfriend. That is my friend's wife."

"So what?"

Knowing how her looks affected men, Margo only smiled. "Let's go, a friend of my husband."

A massive crowd of migrants on the square before *HIAS* moved like an ocean wave. Austrian citizens evaded that crowd, looking with apprehension and discontent.

Margo's beauty attracted people like a magnet and seemed well-known. One after another would come up and pay her compliments—Adam, bewildered, watched men and Margo.

"Listen, Margo, if I ask HIAS to give me my documents ... how may I ask about it?" Adam was distraught. "It's not like asking for a plate with a meal. Please, give me my papers. After all, they could say no! It could be an answer."

"Well, most importantly, don't give up. Oh, do not move. Say nothing, and don't turn around! Stay still." Margo grabbed Adam's arm.

"Lord! What happened?"

"Here comes Caruso. Do not talk with him."

"Who is Caruso?"

"Shut up," shushed Margo, and she turned toward the approaching man.

"Hi, beautiful Margo!" came the man's familiar greeting.

"Who is that guy? He looks like Honore de Balzac."

"This is Adam. He is Igor's friend from Leningrad."

"Listen, Balzac. Do you have corals beads for sale?"

Adam didn't understand anything about corals but shook his head, just in case. Caruso lost interest in him, and with a familiar glance at Margo, he went looking for other prey.

"What was that all about? Is his name *Caruso* for real?"

"No, of course not. His name is Vladik. His nickname is Caruso; he received it in Odessa, singing in restaurants.

He's a real gangster, and he's very shameless. Please stay away from him. Okay, it's time for you to go. I'll wait for you here."

Adam went to the door of *HIAS*, joining the circulating flow of people entering and leaving the building, crowded in the corridor in long lines.

"Who is the last?"

"I am," replied a small, skinny older man with scared eyes.

"Will it take a long time?"

The older man turned out very talkative and quickly explained the situation to Adam.

"No, it goes very fast. You'll need to give them the address you have lodged here, and they will send you to Italy in ten days."

"I'm not going to Italy. I need to stay here in Vienna."

The older man got scared. He raised his eyebrows and retreated as if Adam could infect him with something dangerous.

" They can throw you out. And then what would you do?"

"I don't know. But I need to stay." Adam shivered.

"Well, if you have to stay, so it should be. I wish you the best of luck."

The older man headed to an available worker at the table, and Adam went to the next one.

"Sit. Last and first name. Where are you staying? Do you know the procedure?"

The company representative of *HIAS* spoke Russian but with a heavy accent.

"Everyone is going to Italy, but I want to stay in Vienna."

Adam's words made the wrong impression on the *HIAS* man. He was irritated and said dryly, "We've not handled immigration in Austria. You have to go to Italy. Bye."

"Just give me the documents, and I'm gone."

"You don't get any documents. Goodbye, mister ... uh ..." He looked at the paper. "Mr. Gardov."

Adam left *HIAS* very upset and retold the story to the waiting Margo.

"Don't get upset," she tried to calm him down. "Tomorrow, we'll go again. We'll fight them until they surrender. They have to give you the documents."

"And if not, what then? What money should I live on?"

"Go to *Rav Tov*, as we did. Don't worry; everything will be okay."

But in the rest of the days that followed, Adam worried. If *Rav Tov* changed their mind, he would be thrown out. He was in a foreign country without money or assistance. People were respectful to *HIAS* and almost prayed to this office, and what had he said? *Give me the documents! I must think about my cocky, lewd, and rude behavior toward HIAS. They try, they work hard, and instead of thanking them, I said, "I will do much better without you."*

The following day, history repeated itself. Margo came to the Danau and then waited for Adam in the square while he spoke with *HIAS* employees. The result proved to be unexpected.

"This means you, Mr. Gardov, can do without our money? Here are the documents. Perfect, perfect. Go away, do wherever you want to do."

Adam was stunned, happy, and confused at the same time. Margo was happy to see Adam with a bundle of papers, and she dragged him away.

"That's all. We've done it. Let's go back to the Danau. You can show them to Igor in the evening and then go to Rav Tov with the papers."

But things happened in an unexpectedly different way. Adam had barely crossed the hotel's threshold when an administrator called him to a desk.

"I'm sorry, but Madam Betina called and said you are being evicted from the hotel."

"How, why? Where am I going to stay?"

The administrator sympathetically spread his hands and gave Adam a handset.

"Call Igor."

Adam dialed the number. His fingers and his voice quivered.

"Igor, hi! Madam Betina ordered to evict me from the Danau."

"Yeah, I'm aware of that. *HIAS* demanded it."

"What do I do now?"

"Take your suitcase, and go to another hotel. You'll stay overnight there. They're expecting you. Write down the address; for God's sake, don't get caught by Madam Betina. Tomorrow morning, we will go to *Rav Tov*. And do not panic. All problems can be solved."

Adam was accepted and taken into a utility room at the specified address. He spent the night full of despair and doubt, horrified by what he had done.

What have I done? "*Well, then, you are not pleased with Italy? We'll see, in Vienna, he wants to stay with friends. Is it not enough for a poor emigrant?*" *And if the Rav Tov does not take me under its wing? Will I return with repentance to HIAS again to beg for Italy? Yes, in such a case, I will be sent to hell but not to Italy! And they would be right. What the hell was I thinking before?*

Adam tossed, turned, and cursed his stupidity. He spent the whole night like this and only fell into a short sleep in the morning.

Vienna—Night Fears

A KNOCK AT THE DOOR AWAKENED HIM.

"*Bitte! Bitte*, telephone!"

Adam was sleepy but hastily dressed and approached the administrator's desk. The voice on the phone politely addressed him in German. "*Herr* Adam, bitte."

"Hello?" he muttered, startled. He was not expecting anything good from this call.

"Well, finally, it's you. Hi, this is Igor. Grab a taxi, and get to the Zum Turken right now. Give the phone to the administrator."

Adam held out the phone. The administrator listened to Igor, said, "Bitte," and then proceeded to call somewhere. Adam silently waited until he turned to him with another "Bitte."

"Bitte, Herr Adam, taxi, bitte."

Adam automatically answered "Bitte" and walked out into the street.

I should have said to Danke, *"Thanks." Why did I tell him, bitte? Isn't it the same as,* please?

Adam had been taught German at school, which popped into his memory as separate words. He could not create phrases but could say "hello" and "thank you."

"Good news!" Igor greeted him.

"What? I'm deported to Russia?"

"You're what? No, all is okay. Madam Betina got a new hotel for migrants and needs a worker there."

"And what have I to do with it?"

"I recommended you, and she agreed. You're going there to work and live. Ilya will be here soon. We are going to the *Rav Tov* right now. It's all worked out perfectly, buddy."

Adam couldn't believe his luck. A moment ago, he was desperate and had no idea what to do. Suddenly, all was solved.

"Igor, I am in your debt for the rest of my life."

"C'mon, we are friends. Oh, Ilya, hey! Well, Adam, we can go."

The rabbi from *Rav Tov* met them as though they were old friends. He took the documents *HIA*S had issued, gave Adam his monthly allowance, and invited Adam to go to the warehouse to choose as many used clothes as he would like. Adam could not calm down and admired his warm welcome at *Rav Tov*.

"Look, it's just business," explained Igor. "And like any other business, it requires a good relationship with the client. By the way, *'Rav Tov'* translates as 'good rabbi.'"

When they returned to the Zum Turken, there was Madam Betina. She went directly to Adam and quickly spoke. "Igor explained everything to you?"

"Yes. Thank you very much, Madam Betina."

"Ride to *Die Damen von Madam*. Check out the rooms, meet with the manager, and return immediately. We'll settle a new group of migrants there in the evening."

Capital of Immigrants

She turned to Igor and Ilya, giving orders and speaking rapidly and overbearingly.

Adam kept thinking, *What is it, Die Damen von Madam? And how will I speak with the manager?*

When Madam Betina left, he looked at Igor, puzzled.

"I don't speak German," said Adam.

"And who says now life will be easy? You'll manage."

"And this *Die Damen*—is it something like Zum Turken and Danau? Or is it classier? The name sounds strangely familiar."

Ilya and Igor looked at each other and laughed.

"Have I said something funny? Why do you laugh?"

"Adam, it's the most famous whorehouse in Vienna!"

"A whorehouse? Are you serious?"

"Of course, I'm serious. Dames from 'Madam.'"

"And how should I settle migrants in a place with prostitutes?"

"Not with them, of course. In one half of the hotel, prostitutes live and work, and on the other side will be migrants."

"What a nightmare!"

"It's how you look at it. In Vienna, there is no housing for rent. From morning to evening, Madam Betina is looking for housing for migrants. The Austrians do not want to let Russians be guests. Russians act like barbarians, pulling out fixtures they need, unscrewing lightbulbs, removing plumbing and mirrors, and unscrewing sockets. And you're talking about a whorehouse?"

* * *

On the outside, *Damen von Madam* looked decent and fashionable. Adam showed a spread of fingers to a taxi driver and added,

"Fünf minuten, bitte!" (five minutes, please). The driver nodded knowingly and turned off the engine.

My German is good. I've broken the language barrier.

Inside, it was dimly lit. There stretched a long corridor; on the right of the main entrance, a small window from some office in a wall sat a big fellow with a stone face. Adam mentally called him *"SS"* and said aloud, "Bitte, Madam Betina."

The *SS* man scowled and gestured to Adam to follow him. There was a long corridor. Finally, the big man stopped in front of a wide-open door. Behind a bar sat two women wearing only panties and bras. Adam swallowed and looked. The man crooked his finger.

"Du kannst nicht in die Bar gehen. Du kannst nicht nach links gehen. Du verstehst?" asked *SS* menacingly. *"Going to the left is impossible. Going to the bar is forbidden."* Adam understood. *"Verstehen, verstehen."* (I understand.) *What was not to understand?*

A staircase right off the bar led upstairs, with only one room. The guide pointed at the door and roughly poked Adam in the chest. *"Bitte, Wohnen."*

So, it's understandable. My housing is sorted out. But where will I be lodging a horde of migrants?"

He followed the man to the next floor with a long corridor and doors on both sides.

"Wohnen." Please, for you (to stay).

"Ya, ya, ich verstehen." (Yes, yes, I understand.)

The tour ended. The *SS* man turned and strode down the steps. Adam did not lag, and on the way back, he only glanced at the girls behind the bar.

Why are they so skinny? It's scary. They are not like Russian whores.

The SS man plopped behind his desk and turned his back to Adam.

"Auf Wiedersehen," Adam said goodbye, having just remembered another German expression from his school vocabulary. The man did not respond.

* * *

In the Zum Turken, he told Igor and Ilya that he got acquainted with the best whorehouse in Vienna, and all three had a good laugh. Soon a new batch of migrants came with Madam Betina. She greeted the aides and stiffly nodded at Adam.

He wanted to cringe but smiled in reply.

Now, everything depends on her. I will do whatever she wants. And God forbid if she doesn't like my work. She could kick me out or forget me, saying, "What was the name of ..."

Ilya and Igor started work; they signed in the newcomers, paid out money, and distributed temporary residences. Adam carefully watched and studied. He might soon do the same job and have to avoid looking like an idiot.

When Madam Betina speedily disappeared to solve other tasks, Igor invited the migrants to sell vodka, caviar, and champagne. Some did not even reply. Igor looked at Ilya, and he took up the handset.

"Hello! Hotel Zum Turken, bitte. *Drei taxi ... ya, ya, zusammen. Danke schoen.*"

I wish I could speak more German; Ilya ordered three taxis to arrive together.

Adam thought, listening to the confident speech of his friend and watching as people fussed, grabbed belongings, and poured into the street. Igor had to answer many questions: "Where are we going? What place? Is it convenient? How far is the center?"

"You'll see."

After escorting the group, Igor came back and exhaled heavily. "Uff! Groups from Moscow. That is always a problem."

Adam did not understand.

"It was a plane from Moscow," Igor explained.

"I realized that. And what isn't right?"

"Everything. Wait—you will get acquainted with that. Those migrants from Moscow and the people from Leningrad always have a bunch of claims and problems. And there are always demands and complaints." Ilya nodded, agreeable.

"People from Odessa are very different. They only want apartments with kitchens. Migrants offer us things to sell, and they all know prices better than we do."

Betina appeared again. "Is all well?"

"Yes, Madam Betina. All were sent. No problems."

She turned to Adam. "In the evening, you'll take the first batch. Did you already go there?"

"Yes, I looked at everything, Madam Betina."

"All should go gently and very quietly."

"Of course, Madam Betina. I understand."

"Your salary is eighty schillings a month. Do you have questions?"

"No. Thank you, Madam Betina."

She nodded and disappeared.

"Congrats!" Igor slapped Adam on the shoulder, taking that as his adoption into the circle.

"Your group will arrive three hours from now. We have time to grab a bite and relax. Let's go prepare the feast while Ilya writes the report."

They pulled a cloth onto the table in a small room that served as Ilya's home and a delicacies warehouse. Igor brought a loaf of bread, some tomatoes and set the table up with a bottle of vodka, a jar of caviar, sprats, and some other fish in tomato sauce.

"We are living beautifully." Adam grinned.

"Of course! Would you live near the river and have no water to drink? Get plates, cups, and forks. They are there at the bedside table."

"So, I understand you guys buy products from migrants, and then it is resold?"

"No, that has all been eaten and drunk."

"Excuse me. I said it without thinking."

"I'm joking. Call Ilya."

Ilya came; at the sight of the prepared table, his eyes shone, and he poured the vodka into glasses. Adam also realized that he was starving and wanted to drink.

"Well, there you go. For your first day." Igor raised a toast.

"Guys, I'm so thankful. No words can describe it. And I will have a paid salary. I can't believe it."

"It's not the salary, some petty cash fund. For such money, none of the local labor will do."

Ilya filled the empty glasses with vodka and looked at the upper tier of beds.

"But there is an opportunity to earn."

They laughed. Thanks to Ilya, a great alcohol lover, the bottle quickly emptied. He yawned and said, "That's it, guys. I will sleep, and you are on duty."

Igor and Adam returned to the hall and found the hotel buzzing like an anthill. Many suitcases were in the hall. Men and women were running between the rooms and the lobby. Some waited with bags in hand, ready for any developments. They were moving toward the desk, with much noise. A child was crying bitterly. Adam heard snatches of a family quarrel.

"Where's the kid's stuff? I wrapped it separately."

"In a suitcase that was removed?"

"You are so stupid! Get it right away. I said *now*."

Adam quietly asked Igor, "What happened?"

"I don't have a clue. The large group is leaving for Italy today, but—hey, people, calm down! What is that noise, and why are there fights? Why are you making so much fuss? Taxis will be here in forty-five minutes."

"But we were told it would be right now."

"Who said that?"

"It's not important now. Someone said it."

"Stop panicking. A taxi will come later. You have time to eat."

Men, quietly cursing, went out on the street to smoke. Women were trying to find out who had spread the panic.

Finally, the taxis arrived, and the uproar began again. People jostled, treading on each other's heels, and tried to squeeze through to the exit first.

Just like in the good old days, thought Adam.

Igor shouted to the crowd, "Citizens, take turns! The transport will not leave until everything is settled. There will be enough places; don't worry. Every car can take four people. No, three cannot go; look for a fourth. Softly, softly. You will not be separated; you only go to the train station."

With shouts and lots of noise, people finally settled into the taxis. Igor paid the drivers and collected receipts. There were finally sounds of people saying, "Thank you, thank you!"

"Goodbye! Happy migration!"

Igor and Adam waved to the leaving migrants. The cavalcade moved, and Igor returned with Adam to the hall. Adam glanced at his watch. "Is Ilya still asleep?"

"Oh yes. He loves to drink. He will sleep until we wake him. Soon your group will come. This group was transported through the Chop border point; keep that in mind. The group will be divided; we will keep about twenty people here. You'll take the rest to the brothel. Are you nervous?"

"Honestly? Very much."

"Not to worry; it's only scary the first time." Igor was encouraging. "It will be nice. You'll see."

Damen Von Madam

LATE AT NIGHT, the buses with migrants came. People looked tired and stressed from the long, hard road but were happy. Madam Betina, as expected, congratulated all the arrivals to the free world.

"Gentlemen, heads of the families, come to the desk—approach individually. Tell your family name and the first names of all family members, and get the money," announced Ilya.

The husbands of the families lined up in a single line and, after receiving allowances, were returned to their relatives. Adam noticed that the money immediately passed into the wives' hands, voluntarily or under pressure.

"Now we will decide who will live where. Do any of you wish to stay here in Zum Turken?" Igor asked the crowd.

A forest of hands shot up.

"It's good. Anyone with children comes first. So, how many do you have in your family? I'll make a list."

"We all are here."

"It's clear. Adam, take them into the first room."

Adam quickly returned. "They asked for bed linen."

"Not now … after we finish with resettlement. Show this family a second room, and show those with young children into the third."

Capital of Immigrants

More than half of the group lodged in Zum Turken.

"Igor, there is no more space available."

"Well, pass through the rooms, and invite all here."

"What about the rest? They will go where?" Adam was worried about the group that was not yet settled.

"Now, all will gather, and I'll explain what's next. Don't worry; nobody will be left homeless. So, is everyone here? I have an announcement. We certainly know that everyone brought the so-called *migrants' set*: vodka, caviar, champagne, coral beads, different nesting dolls, and other souvenirs to sell. There were previous cases when police arrested migrants for selling things without licenses. There were severe fines. We will help you guys solve this issue without problems.

"The prices you know from the letters of your friends and relatives. We are ready to buy your products at these prices right now."

"That's great." People were happy. Someone talked to his wife: "I did wonder how, without knowing the language, we would make this sale. To whom would we sell it?"

People rushed to their luggage and brought bottles and cans to the desk.

"Adam, help," ordered Igor.

Igor took the products, Ilya paid cash, and Adam placed the goods on the bed's upper tier. After half an hour, the trade was finished. Igor turned to the group. "So, now about housing. We have new and very nice hotel rooms; they are small—for three to four people. You should never cook or make noise in that hotel, but it is in the city's heart. Adam is always there; you can ask him for anything you need. If you are ready, Adam will take you there by taxi."

The group went outside as the taxis approached.

Adam commanded, "Put your things in the trunks. Four people in each taxi."

On the way, the newcomers stared at the Vienna night sights. The women admired the view.

"It is so beautiful here with all those lights."

The cars pulled to the lighted entrance, letting off the passengers and luggage. People gathered around Adam.

"Please, quietly, get closer to me. I should clarify something. Firstly, this place is called Damen von Madam, translated as 'Ladies from Madam.' First, you can't cook here. You need to keep quiet and behave … hmm, delicately. That is a brothel where prostitutes work legally."

"This is a brothel? Seriously?" wondered one of the men.

"Are you crazy?" One of the women got upset. "I have a baby, and here are prostitutes! Ugh, my Lord, I do not believe this."

"And what do we do? Live directly among whores?"

"No, no," explained Adam hurriedly. "We have a separate corridor with rooms on the second floor. All the rooms are clean and decent. The prostitutes live in the left wing of the house, and we are staying on the right wing; we will not interact with them. Further, do not go to the left half. Now, let's not have trouble; do not use the manual electric heater to boil water for tea. If you turn them on simultaneously, the electricity will go out, immediately becoming clear who is to blame. They could evict you or take away your appliances. None of you would want that.

Do not take anything from the bar or communicate with the ladies. Even with money, you can't. And you don't have enough money to walk around the bars. Here's another point: Vienna is full of dishonest dealers who buy goods from migrants. I know that many of you still have things for sale. I will tell you with whom you can deal and from whom it is better to stay away. You are adults and are responsible for yourselves. I can only warn you against stupid steps. My room is on the floor below. If you have questions, do not hesitate to contact me. Tomorrow at nine in the morning, everyone comes down to this same place; we have to go and register with *HIAS*. And now go quietly behind me. I'll show you to your rooms."

Adam picked up a suitcase and went to settle in his room after settling his group. It was comfortable with all amenities. He took a shower, and for the first time in many days, he fell asleep quickly.

* * *

Feeling responsible for the people entrusted to him, Adam went down early in the morning and joined his compatriots. The entire group was already waiting for him on the street.

"How did you sleep last night? Hopefully, nobody bothered you. That's good. I will take all of you to *HIAS*; you can sign up and get some money there. Then you will be free until you get on a train to Italy."

Adam took the people onto the sunny streets of Vienna. Before the jewelry store, the crowd stood in disbelief. People admired the store with delight and surprise, looking at the goods exhibited.

"Oh, my God! Is it all real?"

Adam realized the impression such sights had on the migrants. He had just wondered about it two days ago; he couldn't believe all these treasures were publicly displayed. Even in Leningrad's famous chain of stores, Gostiny Dvor, with their enormous glass storefronts, he had never seen anything like it. An older man, who had come from the province, shook his head and mumbled in admiration.

"Well, here is the wealth. And we fools lived there and knew nothing."

"People, come on; there will still be time to admire it later."

As always, the square in front of HIAS was crammed with people. Adam talked to his group. "People, I say goodbye for now to you. Get in line to *HIAS*, and whenever you have finished, return to the hotel."

"Hey, Balzac." Adam's blood ran cold. "Cool, Balzac. I've heard you now work for Madam Betina and care for Damen von Madam."

"Hi, Vladik. Who told you that?"

"Rumors spread quickly here. Look at you—growing fast. I'll be there tonight."

"Listen, Vladik—"

"Call me Caruso."

"Well, Caruso, explain why I should help you?"

"Balzac, I think you're insolent."

"I'm not. It's a simple question: how do I benefit from helping you?"

"Yes, you are a smart guy. But I like it. Okay, I'm convinced. I'll pay you 10 percent of the goods price of whatever I buy. However, wait until the evening."

Adam exhaled.

Wow! If Caruso agrees, the others, who buy goods from migrants, will also agree.

He went to the café with the nice grilled chicken. He ate half a chicken, leaving the other half for later.

Among other things, it's a clever idea for small businesses. Maybe in America, I will organize such a café. I can do all the work myself, Adam thought, returning to Damen von Madam.

He constantly thought about making a living in the United States, which increasingly worried him. He didn't speak accurate English. He must study it every day, using tutorials and dictionaries.

But so many things had happened in the last few days. Studying is hard when so many problems happen at the same time. Time leaks through my fingers. I must learn English daily. I must start immediately.

Adam stepped over the threshold of the hotel. The SS man, as always, was sitting at his post. He was sullen and silent.

"*Guten tag.*" Adam smiled broadly. He did not expect a reply to his greeting; he just enjoyed watching the face of the rude manager each time Adam showed him a courtesy in German.

At his door, he found a standing, short, Eastern-looking guy.

"Hello. My name is Janek. I hear you're the senior here. Can I be your friend?"

"Why is that?" Adam was surprised.

"I buy cigars, preferably Churchill, and other kinds that come my way. I know I must give you 10 percent of the purchases. It suits me."

Wow, how quickly rumors spread. The house is barely settled, and people already know the interest rates. Adam was surprised.

"A few people are here working with migrants," continued Janek, as if answering the question. "Those who purchase goods from migrants know each other."

"And where did you come from?"

"I'm from Tashkent, Uzbekistan. I know you are from Leningrad, yes?"

Adam liked this guy. "Okay, Janek, come in the evening. I will ask if people have cigars."

"Maybe people will have Churchill cigars? Those are the best-selling ones. I will pay a top price."

"Understood. Come back about eight o'clock."

Cigars? It's something new. There were many Cuban cigars in Russia, which were cheap because nobody smoked them. But it turns out there is a demand. So, okay, Adam, let's go forward. The future is waiting. Must study English.

All the migrants gradually returned to the hotel. They were already somewhat comfortable and cheerfully walked into their rooms, carefully not noticing the scantily clad girls at the bar. When they had all returned from HIAS, Adam tapped the doors of the rooms and called them into the corridor.

"In the evening, we will have guests named Caruso and Janek. You can sell your things but don't sell them too cheaply. If you don't know the prices, call me. Does anyone have Cuban Churchill cigars?"

"I have. But I do not sell it cheaper than twenty-five dollars per box."

"Well, that is good. Please, learn from that man and do not sell too cheap. And keep your eyes open."

Caruso came first.

"How are we doing, Balzac?"

"Everything is okay. I have warned everyone. So, people are waiting for you."

"Well done, Balzac. I see that I can deal with you." He went upstairs.

Janek showed up.

"Wait, Janek, Caruso is there now."

Adam stopped him, and Janek immediately wilted.

"Come back in forty minutes. There is a box of Churchills for twenty-five dollars."

"Excellent, Adam, thank you! I'll drop by later. I don't want to meet with Caruso. He's such a—"

"Yeah, yeah, I know."

Caruso came down after half an hour but didn't look very happy. "Balzac, something wrong happened."

"Well, they were in the Zum Turken and sold most of their stuff."

"I understand. I worked there but did not get along well with Madam Betina; she preferred Ilya. I couldn't care less. I'm going to Paris soon. I'll be singing in a restaurant, Rasputin."

"Great! I have heard that this is one of the most expensive restaurants. I envy you."

"And you're right, Balzac. Well, look. I bought coral beads and a famous Palekh jewelry box. Altogether, it was one hundred schillings. Here are ten, and be healthy."

Adam thanked him and looked at Caruso, who drank beer from a bottle. How would he check to see how many goods he had bought? Well, at least he got ten schillings.

Janek soon returned.

"Is Caruso gone?"

"Gone, gone. The road is free."

Janek went upstairs to the residents and then returned twenty minutes later.

"Here, Adam, I bought a box of cigars and souvenirs. Altogether, it was thirty dollars, so you get $3, or forty-two schillings." He handed Adam the money and said goodbye.

Adam counted his earnings: fifty-two schillings.

He would not get rich, but he would not be hungry. All in all, it was not bad on the first day.

Adam finished the chicken remnants and had hot tea with biscuits. He sat down with an English book to conquer the table of irregular verbs.

"Be, was, were, been ..."

Suddenly, a loud knock on the opened door forced Adam to forget his English and Russian.

"Hi. Are you Adam?"

"Uh, yes. Yes, enter."

"We are already here."

A man and a woman stood in the doorway, beautiful, young, and very confident. Adam, alarmed, sensed something disturbing about them.

"I'm Misha. And this is my wife, Sofia. We are from the city of Odessa."

Capital of Immigrants

It's understandable; they don't have to say that. People from that town are well known for their self-certainty.

In the meantime, Misha continued, "We're buying goods from migrants. My wife recently learned about your commission price for representing buyers to migrants. So, you can represent us to migrants."

Despite Adam's doubts, something in Misha's voice compelled him to help these guests. At that time, neither he nor anyone else knew that it was *Misha Steamer,* a future VIP of the famous New York district of Brighton Beach. Adam presented new buyers to migrants and returned to his room to wait and see with concern what this business couple would buy. Perhaps they could persuade people, as they had brought down an impressive package stuffed with purchased goods.

"The whole catch of today was one hundred forty schillings," said Misha. "Do you want to check?"

Adam didn't want to. Something told him that it would be a bad idea to check. He had better take Misha's words.

"Here are fourteen schillings. We'll check with you from time to time," promised Misha.

"I'll be happy," lied Adam.

They had hardly left the doorway when a cleaning woman in uniform appeared.

"Herr Adam, phone, bitte."

"Danke schoen."

"Pozhalusta." (Please.) *She spoke in broken Russian.*

"Oh, you speak Russian?"

"Ne'mnozh'ko is Yugoslavia." (Little bit; from Yugoslavia.)

"Oh, you speak little. Good!"

"I clean here the—" she lowered her voice, *"kurvochkam."* Adam understood this word in Russian, meaning women in such professions.

"And do you clean our wing too?" Adam, already at the door, asked.

"Only when people leave, and new ones come."

"Got it, *spasibo.*"

"Sure." She smiled.

Adam hurried down; the phone was on the nasty *SS* man's dark desk. He slid back part of the glass window and silently gave Adam the handset.

"Hello?"

"Hi, this is Igor. Can you come to the Zum Turken right now?"

"Oh, what happened?" Adam was worried.

"Come over. I will tell you."

In the taxi, Adam pondered why he was suddenly needed. He did not like it when he was suddenly called; he expected trouble.

* * *

Igor met him, slyly squinting. "We have an order for our goods. But I'm supposed to be here. Can you help Ilya go there and make a delivery?"

"Lord, of course! For God's sake, next time, don't scare me. I can always do whatever you need, but don't make me crazy with fear."

"Sorry, I did not think. Okay, go help Ilya; he's packing the goods."

In the room, Ilya worked at full speed. The quilt was open from the second-tier beds. Jars, bottles, and gifts were transferred into four huge bags but could not be closed. Adam and Ilya tried to stow the goods differently; it was impossible.

"Maybe we should leave the champagne?"

Adam was ready to give up.

"Better we leave some of the vodkas. The New Year is soon; champagne will fly out fast."

Half an hour later, they took their laden bags and exited the taxi in front of the back entrance to a big building resembling a theater. They met a youthful, good-looking man who greeted them and led them to get in, casually saying to the guards, *"Zusammen."*

Together, understood Adam.

They walked for a long time until they arrived somewhere behind the scenes. There Ilya pulled out some champagne bottles and a few bottles of vodka and counted twenty cans of black caviar. Their guide recorded something on paper, handed Ilya the money, and walked them out.

"Goodbye." He smiled. "Thanks, Ilya. I'll call you again."

Adam could not restrain himself when they had empty bags on the street.

"Who is this guy? An actor? The administrator? Where did he learn Russian?"

"He and some other people there are Russians. I have no idea who runs the theater. He sometimes buys the products. They do not encourage asking questions here. Let's go. We have more customers."

Soon they faced another back entrance, this time in a big shop. Ilya pressed the doorbell, and they were admitted. A tall young man who spoke German met them. Ilya answered without any problem, and Adam regretted that he understood nothing of their conversation. They started negotiating to sell the goods, and soon Ilya got a bundle of crisp bills.

When they left the store, Ilya seemed happy.

"We have to sell some souvenirs. Let's go fast before the store closes. The bags are light now."

They were passing the storefront of a big store. Adam looked in the window and suddenly stopped.

"Look, Ilya; caviar is the same as we have. It's seven hundred fifty schillings per jar. The markup is crazy."

"These are the rules of the game." Ilya shrugged.

They entered the strange store. The gift store with Russian goods in the window looked like a junk dealer's warehouse. There were glass showcases with Russian medals, wood-covered boxes with drawings, lacquered boxes, folk handicrafts, souvenirs, fur hats, downy shawls, and military officers' caps.

"What nice guests! And without an escort. Anyone from the hotel Zum Turken is always welcome." An old, fat man in a Russian embroidered shirt grinned widely, exposing yellow horse teeth. "Well, friends, give me your jewelry. Ilyusha, where are all the nice goods? Are the people impoverished, or do I have competitors?"

"Neither one. You know we have lucrative days, and there are empty ones."

"Ilyusha, don't tell me tales. I've been in this business for so many years. Why do I need this merchandise? Look how much of this junk is around. Where are the jewelry, coral beads, old lacquer boxes, icons?"

"Yes! I know, but not yet. You will be the first to know when we get some," promised Ilya.

"Oh, and how much do you want for this junk?"

He sighed mournfully.

While trading, Adam considered the murky glass display, which, like museum storage, held things of past times.

"Well, young people, it has been a while. Don't forget the old man." They went over the threshold, and Adam grimaced. "He's a disgusting type."

"Yes, a real miser. He is not squeamish; he will buy smuggled or confiscated goods. Why does he bother? He lives alone. When he dies, everything goes to the ashes."

They returned to the hotel, where Igor waited on them.

"Well, finally, you guys came back. I was getting worried. How was the sale? Is everything okay?"

"Of course. It would be much better to be less excited and place some food on a table."

"I finished preparing the meal a long time ago. I've only been waiting for you."

"Oh, again, this migrants' set."

Ilya grimaced, seeing the familiar table with the well-known assortment.

"You, sir, are snickering." Igor guffawed. "People dream of black caviar and Stolichnaya vodka. However, there are surprises. I asked someone to cook a borscht with a nice piece of beef for us. It's ready and still on the stove. Let us drink the first shot. To a good, profitable day, guys."

The borscht proved to be excellent. It was spicy and aromatic, rich, with a large piece of meat—an authentic Ukrainian meal.

After returning to the Damen von Madam, Adam reminisced about it almost with a taste in his mouth; it was a fantastic delicacy. He thought it necessary to include borscht in his future New York restaurant menu.

Zum Turken

THE WEEK WENT QUIETLY. Adam helped migrants solve their more pressing daily problems, but he mostly sat over his textbooks. His English still left much to be desired, but his persistence and tenacity could be envied. Everyone who walked past the room's open door always saw him with a dictionary in his hands. By the end of the week, a rumor reverberated through Die Damen von Madam that he was fluent in the language. And it looked as though the rumor had penetrated the left half of the hotel. Once, on the threshold of his room, appeared a girl. She was not quite sober and had very animated hands.

"Do you speak English? Yes?"

Within limits, Adam could. "Yes, I do."

She closed the door, leaned on it with her back, and let out a tirade in pure English. Adam sat on the bed, bewildered, gaping. He would not understand a word, but from time to time, he would nod.

What does she want? Sex? She makes a living out of it. Communication? But my English is so poor that she had already probably guessed it. Maybe she wants a drink. But I have nothing, and it's obvious.

The girl spoke even faster. Adam painfully listened with attention, trying to hear a familiar word, but the unusual situation and Russian shyness made communication impossible. Finally, she stopped and seemed aware of the failure of her attempts to get through to him.

She was disappointed.

"Auf Wiedersehen." Then she disappeared.

Adam mumbled, "Goodbye," and sighed with relief when she slammed the door.

Oh, these Germans. And what should I do?

The encounter bothered him, and he decided to go for the grilled chicken. Adam felt the mocking looks of half-naked ladies passing by the bar and was vexed.

Well, what are they doing? Do they laugh at me? Or do they constantly review any man?

That also troubled him, and he felt anxiety from the uncomfortable meeting with a representative of their tribe.

Grilled chicken—this, of course, is great. It is juicy with a lot of spices. But I have the same bland food daily, no matter how delicious. I must enjoy Viennese schnitzel. Being in Vienna and not trying is just a crime.

Adam turned the other way but stopped when he heard a familiar voice call out his name. "Hey, hello, Adam! Where are you going?"

Breathless, Janek ran across the street and shook his hand.

"Hi, Janek. You are just in time. I want to try Viennese schnitzel. Do you know how it is different from our Russian food?"

"Yes, I do."

"Listen, you do speak a little German? Come with me; help me order it."

"Okay, Adam, but do you know how much schnitzel costs?"

"No, but we will find out. I want to try it."

They walked down the street searching for inexpensive cafés, looking at menus.

"That one looks good. There are free tables, and it looks normal," advised Janek.

They entered and sat down at the corner table. A waitress handed them menus.

"Janek, look at the menu. Do they have Viennese schnitzel?"

"They do. Dear mother, forty schillings! Let's go and look for another café."

"No, I'll order. I thought it would be much more. And what are you going to have?"

"Nothing. I am saving money for New York. I want to open a small business there."

"Well, at least take a cup of tea. I feel uncomfortable. I'll be eating, and you'll just be looking at me. Come on—I'll pay."

"It's not necessary. I'm used to eating at home with my wife and children, having lunch," replied Janek. He called the waitress.

"Wir wollen ein Wiener Schnitzel bestellen." (We want to order one Vienna schnitzel).

"Ya," replied the waitress, "Vienna schnitzel." She added, "Danke."

"Janek, you ordered me a schnitzel. Great, you speak good German."

He shrugged. The waitress brought the order in about ten minutes: a huge schnitzel, the size of the entire plate. There was no space for a side dish.

"Wow, now that's a schnitzel!" Adam cut a piece and ate with pleasure. "Listen, it is delicious. And not greasy. Not like what we have in Russia."

"Here, it's made from veal and not from pork."

"Janek, try it. The crust is crispy, and the inside is very juicy."

"Thank you. I believe you. I have a month until I get a visa and finally leave. The truth is, I don't know what I'll be doing in New York. I have a little money, but maybe someone will take me into some business as a partner. And when are you going there?"

"Not soon enough. I also have not yet decided what to do in the United States. Hopefully, I will see you there very soon."

After savoring every bite, Adam ate the schnitzel, and the waitress brought the check.

"Janek, how much of a tip is accepted normally?"

"Give two schillings, and we can go away."

Adam left five schillings without hesitation.

The next day, Adam's first group was leaving for Italy. He commanded everyone to get into taxis, and people said goodbye to him as they would to a good friend. Some stood with tears in their eyes; they were migrants, connected by one fate, and all had been waiting for the unknown and frightening new future. Adam went to Zum Turken to meet with Igor when the people had gone.

Igor looked concerned and started without an introduction.

"Hi, Adam. After one month, American visas will be ready for Margo and me, and we will leave. During this time, we must brush up on our English. We will not pass the medical tests if we do not speak good English. I talked with Madam Betina. She doesn't mind if you work in Zum Turken instead of me. I will send Kolya to your place; he is Misha's man from Danau. Do you understand? That Misha—always wants to get his hands on Zum Turken. Yes, to hell with him; it's not our headache. Kolya will now settle in Damen von Madam. Today you'll sleep in our house, and tomorrow I want to take you to the Diana-Bad, a bath complex with a warm pool, steam rooms, and different procedures."

Adam was stunned by his unexpected promotion but more by the swift departure of his friends.

"I did not think it would happen so quickly, Igor."

"No, but I'll check out a New York situation and help you there when you come."

"Okay! What is a Diana-Bad?"

"As I said, it's a cool bath complex with a warm pool, steam rooms, and different procedures. There is great fun in Vienna."

"I don't even know what to say. How can I ever thank you for everything? You have become like a brother to me."

"Margo and I also have bonded to you. Okay, enough with the sentiments. The New Year will be soon. Some friends will arrange a party with a Christmas tree, homemade food, drinks, and good company—all as it should be. You, naturally, are invited. We will bring the migrants' set—everything else they have. By the way, Margo called her girlfriend, Alla. She's not bad. She has a son of thirteen or fourteen. But for you, does it matter? At least you will not be single on New Year's Eve." Igor winked.

Some young man entered the Zum Turken, looking unmistakably like a migrant. Something in his clothing, behavior, and movement said he belonged to this group.

"Oh, here is a spy from Misha," Igor said quietly and turned to the guy. "Hello. Are you Kolya? Madam Betina is not here; instead, you have me. You will work in Damen von Madam. We are looking forward to a new group of migrants. You'll go with Adam to settle people. He will show you everything."

Igor looked at his watch.

"Adam, wake up Ilya. The cars with people are about to be here."

Soon there was a new party of migrants. Everything went quickly and clearly—the usual scenario.

* * *

Adam explained to Kolya the routine in Damen von Madam.

"Kolya, when we arrive at Damen von Madam, get people off, and I will hold a briefing for the group. Listen carefully, and memorize it. You are going to do it every time with new groups. Just ask me if something is not clear."

"Thanks, Adam. Until now, I have understood all. I was afraid that I would be sent to do everything myself. And who is the owner of that hotel?"

"Some madam. She lives in Switzerland and arrives for money every month. I saw her once, a real lady. And in her absence, all are ruled by a huge, nasty Austrian man. He is spiteful. I call him *SS*. You should be careful with him."

"Oh, how difficult it is. And how do I deal with all this?"

"You can do it; don't worry," reassured Adam. "There is not much of choice."

Diana-Bad

AFTER SETTING PEOPLE AND LEAVING THEM in the care of Kolya, Adam went to Igor's house. Igor greeted Adam warmly and asked about Kolya.

"Normal. Savvy fellow. I think he can do the work without problems. Listen, about Diana-Bad. What if, in the morning, there are new arrivals in the Zum Turken? Can Ilya handle things alone?"

"In the morning shift today, nobody will come. And Ilya won't even notice that we're not there. Surely he befriended a bottle today already and will sleep until lunch."

"He does a lot of drinking," Adam commented.

"Oh, yes. Ilya denies drinking, although Betina has already observed it. She has given him a couple of reprimands. Okay, it's his problem. Margo, we have a guest."

"Hi, Adam! Come, come. Igor, let's get the meal out. Are you hungry? I cooked the meatballs with mashed potatoes. Adam, I heard about your soaring career. With this pace, you will soon become the right hand of Madam Betina."

"Uh-uh, don't jinx it. I'm not dreaming of such a career."

"Well, wash your hands and sit at the table. Just don't make noise; it will awaken my sleeping son."

Capital of Immigrants

"Margo, you're from a fairy tale. Meatballs, potatoes. I would be the happiest man if I had such a wife."

She laughed.

"Did Igor tell you about my girlfriend, Alla, coming to the New Year party? You might even get a chance to make a dream come true."

"I'm not sure if I can do it. Hopefully, I'm going to like her."

Margo closed the kitchen door so as not to disturb the child. At the table, they talked about the future of life in New York and the complex examinations required to confirm the dentists' diplomas. Margo soon went to bed, and the friends sat and made plans to live in a distant, dreamland America. It was long past midnight when Igor summed it up. "Fine, it's time to go sleep; otherwise, we won't get up in time for a bath. Margo prepared the bed for you in the living room."

* * *

In the morning, it was sunny and clear. Diana-Bad was nearby, so they decided to take a walk. The weather and the prospect of Igor's good company pleased Adam.

"Here it is," Igor said, pointing to a large building.

"Wow!" exclaimed Adam. "Looks huge, and there are five floors."

Igor, chuckling, went to the box office for tickets while Adam admired a colossal lobby that exuded cleanliness and order. The two friends went to the men's locker and shower rooms. No one yelled or roared; the children walked calmly and did not run at a breakneck pace.

"Before we go to the bath, we should take showers," mentioned Igor. "This is the German order. After the shower, we'll go everywhere naked."

They entered a room with colossal marble baths, with people already sitting in some.

"Pour hot water and sit in it. Fear not; it's all clean and disinfected."

"Oh, it is wonderful! That is heaven-sent; I'm sitting in heaven. Great! I never expected anything like this. Igor, are we going anywhere else?"

"You'll see."

In the next hall, there were three large swimming pools.

"They have different temperatures," explained Igor. "Cool, warm, and hot. And there is—you see?—the entrance to the sauna. It is dry, not wet or hot, as in Russia, where people beat themselves with branches. Here are no branches from the trees to whip."

There came a whistle. The doors opened, and many heated people jumped out of the saunas.

"Igor, let's go to the sauna."

"Hang on. We go by the whistle. Now we will sit in the pool."

The whistle was heard, and the people poured back into the saunas. Igor and Adam entered too. The doors closed, and they could only see through the small window in the wooden door a man on duty in a white robe who walked and glanced into the windows occasionally to check that everything was okay.

"The doors have closed," explains Igor. "They will open in fifteen minutes."

"And if someone becomes ill?"

"That's why there is a guy on duty. The Germans like exact order," Igor whispered. "Everything goes correctly and follows the rules. When a whistle sounds, the steam rooms will be open. They do not play here. For the Germans, everything should be by order."

The whistle sounded, the doors opened, and everyone rushed to the pools. The two friends had some fun trying different water temperatures in the pools.

"Let's go in the big main pool," offered Igor. "But there, don't go nude. Did you bring swimming trunks?"

"Insulting, man. I picked them up as you told me so."

Men, women, and children splashed in a tranquil swimming pool. But at the sound of a whistle, the pool turned into a raging ocean. Waves rose and fell. With joyful screaming, children dived into the raging artificial waves and popped up like little penguins.

"Well, this is something out of Hollywood." Adam was astonished.

"Yes, the waves run on by the whistle." Igor laughed. "Let's go swim."

They swam in the pool long enough to get tired. After returning to the locker room, the friends changed from their wet swimming trunks and got into clean bathrobes.

"Adam, a wonderful buffet here: beer and lightly salted ham sandwiches. I'm hungry and would have some lunch."

"To beer, honestly, I'm indifferent, but a good sandwich I'll have with pleasure."

The males and females shared the pleasure of the buffet. It was festive. People wore branded white bathrobes. The light beer was decent, and the ham buns were excellent.

"Yes, the place is simple and classy. Thank you, Igor. I want to invite you and Margo here before you guys leave."

"The idea is good, but it's not a cheap exercise. Better to keep the money. You'll need it soon enough.

"Firstly, I would like to invite my real friends. And secondly, let's talk about money. Do you know when your visa will be ready? Yes, and you don't have to leave right away. While the tickets for the plane will be ready, you need to wait a week or two. So, I think you should stay and work in the Zum Turken. And you need money no less than I do. Don't shy away from Madam Betina altogether."

"She will not pay for three of us. And I can't ignore my English study."

"Yes, we'll work in Zum Turken together. As to Betina and her salary, who cares? We do not depend on eighty schillings. Agreed?"

"Well, let's say Ilya will not agree to share the profits from the migrants' sets for three."

"Yes, and God will be with him. We'll divide our share into equal parts. You do have a family, and I'm single. You agree?"

"Okay, I will think and talk to Margo."

New Year's Eve in Vienna

AFTER DIANA-BAD, Adam went to Zum Turken. Ilya was on duty.

"Listen, Adam, now I have to go to my apartment. I haven't been there for a long time. Soon I'll leave for Germany. I have always wanted to live there. You can take my room here. I have collected my things and prepared clean bed linens on the bedside table."

"Wow, thanks, Ilya. What time will you be back to Zum Turken?"

"Whoa, don't rush. Today we are expecting guests from the Israeli agency."

"In honor of what?" asked Adam. "Do they want to persuade migrants to go to Israel?"

"Well, that's a legal reason. But I think they want to buy something tasty for the New Year, and we have exclusive prices on vodka, champagne, and caviar."

"Understood. Ilya, do I have to lay the table for entertaining?"

"Maybe, but nothing particularly now. We will see who's coming and what those guests need from us."

People from the Israeli agency, Sohnut, came at about four p.m. The young man, Jacob, and a young girl, Sara, arrived together. Both of them were former citizens of the USSR. They behaved openly and benevolently and wanted to socialize with migrants. Adam gathered all of them in the lobby.

The speech from the Sohnut representatives was simple rhetoric and did not make an impression on Adam or the other migrants. Jacob did not sound like his colleagues, whom Adam met at the airport. They had spoken with such boorishness at the first meeting when Adam first stepped on Austrian ground. On the contrary, today's guests were truthful and straightforward people who loved Israel. That was their job: meeting, assisting, talking to people, trying to change their decision, and going to Israel. But here, at Zum Turken, was a crowd who had already made a choice. They want to go to the US.

Later, sitting with them at the table, Adam decided to express his opinion after a couple of shots of vodka.

"Guys, I'm sorry, but can I tell you something? Look, I wasn't sure where I wanted to go, maybe to America and perhaps to Israel. I wasn't sure precisely where I wanted to go. When representatives of Israel met me here in Vienna, it became clear to me, *'Welcome back to hell.'* I wanted to escape from the communist 'paradise.' I didn't want to be there. I was greeted with typical Russian rudeness, manners, and appeal to people. And I immediately decided that I did not want to give up my dreams; I wanted to go to America."

"Probably you are right, Adam. But, you know, Israel is a complicated country. Some people have decided, 'Yes, we want to go to Israel.' They will fight for Israel. And for those who are not ready yet, let them go to America."

Capital of Immigrants

After dinner, they asked Adam, "Can we buy vodka, caviar, and champagne from you?"

"It's up to Ilya. Let me call him." He dialed the number. " Ilya, those people want to buy caviar, vodka, and champagne."

"Well, then sell it to them. You know the prices."

"Can I make some discounts? They're like our people."

"To me, they are not. If you want a discount, do it at your own expense."

When the guests from Sohnut left, Adam put aside the money for his partner.

"Ilya here is your share; take it. I did consider it without my percentage."

"Your problem," he remarked wryly. "Igor called me and said he wants to return to work. Then he said you had proposed that."

"Yes, I did."

Ilya looked at him and said, "I prefer if my cut is not changed. I have a half share of the business. And you can share yours as you wish."

"It suits us. I will split my share with Igor."

"It's okay, then. I'm gone, and you're on duty. That's all for today; there will be no arrivals of migrants. If problems appear, call Madam Betina."

There were no problems, and Adam's first night in Zum Turken passed quietly. The following day, Igor came and cheerfully greeted him.

"Hey, Adam! How was your first day on duty?"

"I slept like a baby. Probably yesterday's bath is to blame."

"Listen, Adam; I wanted to say thanks for your offer. Margo and I talked. On the one hand, we need to learn steady

English, so it's not right. We must learn it persistently so we do not fail the exams. And that means I cannot work a full day in Zum Turken. But on the other hand, we do need the money. Every penny counts. It is unknown what things will cost us in New York. We will have to rent an apartment and buy some stuff."

"You are right. You don't know much about the cost of living and what money you'll need, but we will make some in the meantime. In any case, having some extra money is easier than being without it."

By noon, after Ilya appeared, the phone rang. Adam picked it up. "Hotel Zum Turken, bitte! Yes, Madam Betina. Call Ilya? Understood."

He hung up. "She has fourteen people from Moscow. Let's get down to work, guys."

The day was as usual as many previous days, similar to many subsequent days. Most days, a small group of migrants would come from the airport in the morning. In the evenings, big groups would come from train stations. Madam Betina ran around the city searching for available hotel apartments and places. The migrants sat in the lobby of Zum Turken on suitcases and waited to be accommodated. They had a hard time: too many people and little available space.

Finally, the last day of the year came. Visitors today were not expected. It was understood no one would come this night. Ilya stayed voluntarily on duty. Igor and Adam said goodbye to him and went to celebrate their first New Year in exile.

"Igor, what's Ilya going to do tonight?"

"Drinking, as usual, I presume."

Igor shook his head and nodded toward Zum Turken's closed doors.

"What else is there to do on such a night?" Adam agreed.

"So, he is drinking now. Eh, he can drink by himself. I feel sorry for him."

They called the cab and went to see Igor's friends, who were already waiting.

Margo met them, looking great in an unusual dress, elegant hairdo, and a dazzling smile.

"Well, finally! Our son kept asking, 'Where is Dad? Where is Dad?'"

"Give me a kiss, my lovely son."

"We were waiting for you. The old year is already almost gone. According to Russian tradition, we should drink to say goodbye to the old year! Everybody, this is Igor and Adam, and here are the owners of the apartment, Nina and Grisha. Here is Alla, and this is her son, Vitalik," Margo introduced everyone.

They sat around a lovely table; the meal provided looked excellent. There was herring, lightly salted and topped with green onions; hot boiled potatoes and butter; green salad; vegetables; a traditional Russian winter salad called *Olivie* in a large crystal vase; a large plate with cold beef and grated horseradish; pink ham slices; and caviar (black and red salmon roe). It was the traditional Russian holiday table. Everyone was in high spirits.

"People, let's get a drink! Who'll say a toast? Igor, you do it!"

"Okay, okay." He rose.

"Friends, it was a challenging year. All our relatives and old friends remain there in our former homeland. Goodbye to the past. Sometimes it was very unkind and cruel, but in our youth, we remained friends, hoping that all friendships would not change in time. There is only one life, and it quickly passes. That is why we are here. Let's be healthy. In front of us are many crossroads, but we are full of new hope and drink to it. To new, unknown life!"

Nina tried to hold back the tears in her eyes.

"Igor, are you sure you are a doctor rather than a poet? Look, we are all going to cry—such sadness. Have a bite of delicious food, friends. The hot potatoes will get cold."

"Let me get some food for you." Alla turned to Adam. She firmly took the initiative into her own hands. It was evident that she was accustomed to taking command. Adam treated self-confident ladies with some skepticism and caution.

"Alla, give him a herring with potatoes, as Dr. Igor prescribed," suggested Margo.

"And I, as a doctor, can prescribe a vegetable salad with beets because I made it. Who wants the salad from Dr. Margo? By the way, Adam, Nina, and Grisha are also dentists. They decided to stay here in Vienna. We all studied together in medical college. And Igor, Ph.D., taught there."

"So, that's where you met. Igor, did you seduce the students?"

"It was the case," confirmed Igor. "But I was shaking from fear like a freshman on the first date."

"No, it was me shaking from fear." Margo laughed. "Trying to guess why he called me to a meeting."

"And now it is understood. Well, everyone, there are five minutes left before the New Year. Open the champagne, and start the countdown. Hurrah! To the New Year!"

Everyone clinked glasses, drank, kissed, and had fun.

"Igor, let's make another toast. You say it nicely."
"Enough with me. Let Adam do it."
"Ladies and gentlemen—"
"And can you be not so pathetic?"
"Shush, shush. Let him talk."
"Friends! I am grateful to everyone in this room. I met good people this holiday. Our government canceled Christmas, and we had the main holiday only, New Year's. But this day retained all attributes: a Christmas tree, gifts, Santa Claus, and more. This holiday will forever remain the most popular and important in our lives. I don't know how we will meet on the following New Year, but let us hope it passes happily and keeps us smiling."

Toasts followed one after another. They all drank, ate, danced, and laughed until late at night and practically into the early morning. They finally shuffled off to sleep.

* * *

Adam woke up very late, not knowing where he was. In bed, he was not alone. Someone was lying before him, and it was a woman. Adam was surprised to find a feminine breast in his arm. A hot wave struck him.

"Alla," he said quietly, "what are we doing?"

He didn't remember anything. His head buzzed from the drinks. The woman turned her head, and Adam almost fell out of bed. It was Margo; she squinted and slyly reached her lips toward his. Adam responded to the kiss, moaning slightly.

Margo pressed a finger to her lips. "Shh ... let's leave."

They quietly made their way between the other people sleeping side by side. Margo closed the door with a key, and they went out onto the street.

He had always liked Margo and no wonder; this woman was gorgeous. But he had never hinted that he liked her. And here she was! Wishing a friend's wife was taboo.

My God, how did this happen? How could it happen? And where are we going now? Did she plan this? Oh, what do I do now? And where is Igor?

Margo raised her hand, and a taxi appeared. She gave the driver the address and enticed Adam to the back seat.

"Where are we going?"

"My girlfriend gave me the keys to her apartment. You also want this, huh?"

She was inquiring, looking into his eyes. Adam painfully panted and kissed her instead. As soon as they entered the apartment, Adam entered the bathroom and put his head under a stream of cold water. It helped a little, and his consciousness brightened. He glanced in the mirror over the washstand and saw wild, crazy eyes and a red face.

"Adam, what are you doing?"

He resolutely opened the bathroom door. Margo stood in the middle of the room, waiting.

"Forgive me, Margo. I can't. Igor is like a brother to me. I'm sorry."

Then, quickly, almost running, he left the apartment. He strode down the street, and his self-control gradually returned to him. Along with it came pride for his rationality and decency. Regrets about the missed opportunity came much later.

Meetings in Vienna

January was calm. Migrants came and went; the stream of people was consistent. Near the end of the month, the flood of migrants increased dramatically. Many migrants flooded Vienna, and Madam Betina rushed around the city again to resettle people. They lacked housing, and people were nervous. Migrants loudly demanded help and were ready to settle anywhere, even to stay overnight.

On one of those hectic days, an unusual character appeared in the Zum Turken. His behavior, gestures, and manners reminded Adam of a familiar figure from the motherland in his most unsightly arrogant manner. He barely appeared in the hotel's doorway and presented himself to Igor and Adam, looking at the disparaged, tired people sitting on suitcases.

"Ernest Ash. I'm a correspondent for the newspaper *Komsomolskaya Pravda* and a scriptwriter. You've probably seen movies based on my scripts. I need separate housing and normal conditions for work. And quickly. I also brought black caviar. How much will I get for it?"

All sorts of personalities appeared in Zum Turken, but this was Adam's first meeting someone like this. That person clearly did not understand where and who he was now. Convincing this man that he was just like the rest was useless, just as telling him that his services to the Communist Party and the state were irrelevant here. Instead, it was the contrary: the image of the adherent to socialism and his relation to the union of the Komsomol, the communist youth organization, was inappropriate here. Igor took on the thankless task of educating Comrade Ash.

"Ernest, you see, this is *another* country. And the rights of migrants are all equal. Now, we have problems with housing. There are too many newcomers; places for all are lacking. First, we care for families with children and then look after the rest."

"You are working badly. You do not understand at all. And look at the fact that people have no choice and should suffer because of your incompetence. What's your profession?"

Ash was arrogant.

"I'm a doctor."

"You should know how to treat people in stressful situations. I saw that you bought black caviar from others. Why do you ignore my question about it?"

"Because, dear Ernest, they have caviar packed in jars."

"So, what?"

"Yours is in a cup; it's useless to anybody."

"What am I supposed to do with it?"

"Eat it. Caviar is perfect for you."

Adam saw that Igor was barely restraining himself from spitting in the face of this stupid boor, so he quickly came up to Igor and whispered, "For God's sake, send this reporter somewhere. He is just a bloodsucker."

"I have no place for this type of person. We are waiting to see if Madam Betina can find some available places."

Ilya, Adam, Igor, and others gathered in the hall, silently staring at the *Komsomolskaya Pravda* newspaper correspondent. The man raised his head, ignoring the icy waves of scorn, and proudly strode to the exit, having muttered through his teeth at parting, "You will hear about me."

A week later, Igor's family received US visas. A goodbye gift from him was a three-room apartment, which Adam inherited.

"Rav Tov pays all the bills, thank goodness." Igor smiled. "They don't mind if you stay where Margo and I had."

Adam felt an unpleasant prick at mentioning her name, but he had promised himself to keep quiet about the New Year's Eve happenings, even under torture. His heart thudded as a sign of gratitude.

Soon Igor's family left, and Adam plunged headlong into work to numb the sadness. The benefit was that hard work kept his mind occupied. With Ilya, he barely coped with the enormous crowds of migrants daily. Adam rarely went to his empty apartment. He convinced himself this was due to objective reasons, but he felt lonely. On the other hand, it did not make sense to leave Zum Turken in the middle of the night to hurtle back through the city early in the morning.

After another two weeks, he got a phone call from Igor. "Greetings from NYC! How are you doing, buddy?"

"Mostly the same. The news is that Ilya went to Germany. So, apparently, Madam Betina promoted me in rank to the first mate. I'm drowning with work."

"Okay, don't pretend that you do not enjoy it. And who is working with you?"

"Madam Betina moved Kolya over, and she got someone else for his place in the Damen von Madam."

"Listen, Adam; I got a call from a Moscow friend tearfully pleading for help. Among the newcomers will be the daughter of his friends. Tomorrow the girl will fly to Vienna; she is young and inexperienced. Her parents thought they would all be released together, but no. Her parents were stopped, and now it is a family tragedy. Of course, she will be in Vienna and Zum Turken. Her name is Nata. Help her the best you can, and send her to Italy with some reliable acquaintances. You will have to choose for her. I understood that the girl is quite green and naïve, nineteen years old."

"Of course, don't worry. I'll do whatever I can. How are you guys settled in New York? Is there good housing? What about exams?"

"All is okay. It is cool here; you'll see. Call me when you know the date of your arrival. Margo and I will find you an apartment in our neighborhood, a place nearby. Together we will have more fun."

"It is great. Say hello to all," replied Adam.

The next day, Betina brought the migrants from the Moscow aircraft. Adam saw Nata immediately but decided to talk with her after everyone was settled. After registration and payments, he asked, as usual, if anyone wanted to sell stuff brought from the homeland. People kept quiet. Unexpectedly, the girl pulled out a bottle of vodka and champagne.

"You can buy it?"

"Of course. Come with me."

Adam took her into his room with its bunk bed. "Here is your money, Nata. Is that your name?"

"How do you know?" She looked surprised.

"I was asked to take care of you."

"Who? Ah, probably my mom and dad. I should write them a letter. It's urgent. Where can I buy an envelope and stamps?"

"Yes, I'll help you. But first, people must be distributed to hotels, and your housing question needs to be solved.

Bring your stuff, and wait for me here."

When the migrants were placed in taxis, Adam went to the kitchen, where women were constantly gathered.

"Ladies, I need your help. Can I ask you to help one girl? She needs to buy some stamps and an envelope."

"What kind of girl? Is she your girlfriend, Adam?"

"No, she's still a baby. I was asked to help her."

"Yes, we know these children," said one of the women, laughing. "No problem, I'm going to shop. Call your girl."

Nata returned with a bundle of envelopes and stamps in one hand and some bananas in the other. She ate them with evident pleasure, which often only children experienced from such simple things.

"Nata, you spent all the money you got from the vodka and champagne?"

"Yes, but I can write letters every day with it."

"And what will you eat?"

"Well, I bought bananas."

"That's clear."

She immediately sat down and began to write letters, and Adam looked at her. Responsibility for her had been dumped on his head.

Lord, she's just a youthful and innocent girl. Quite insecure. How could her parents think of sending her alone to migrate?

But they couldn't do anything about the situation. It can break adults coming here; it is not something a child can handle. It would be good to keep her in the Zum Turken. I could keep an eye on and help her. But she is a child who has left home and is not fit for the harsh reality of migration. It could be better to place her in my empty apartment. There's a standard kitchen, bathroom, TV, and all necessary for life."

Later in the evening, Adam took Nata home.

"Come, come. It's my apartment, but I rarely come here. You will stay here for a while. And it will be calmer for you now. Here is your room, next to the bathroom. Please stay in the living room for a few minutes. I have to shower and prepare something to eat. We'll get up early tomorrow; you must go to HIAS. I will ask someone from Zum Turken to take you there."

When Adam got out of the bathroom, Nata was sleeping on the couch.

Should I wake her up or let her sleep?

Adam covered her with a blanket and then left.

* * *

In the morning, Adam prepared breakfast. He understood that if he let Nata choose what to eat, she would probably eat bananas again.

"Nata, wake up. We will leave soon, and breakfast is ready now and hot."

"Oh, did I oversleep? Don't blame me, please."

"Not going to." Adam shook his head. "Go and wash. We will have breakfast."

"Now, now. I'm coming right now."

What could I do? She is a child. I certainly could let her stay in Vienna and watch out for her. But soon I will be going to the USA. No, I must send her to Italy. I should find a reliable, good family, migrants, and ask them to look after her there. Otherwise, the girl could be lost. It's so bad. Who am I now? I'm not her father. But Igor asked me to help.

"I'm ready, Adam. We can go. Tell me, what should I do at HIAS?" asked Nata.

"You'll tell them that you live in the Hotel Zum Turken. You'll be registered and get some money for a week. They will give you your appointed date of departure to Italy."

"To Italy, so soon? That's great! I should write to Mom and Dad."

At Zum Turken, Adam first went to the kitchen. The team of women was at full strength.

"Ladies, is anyone going to HIAS today?"

"Is it better to go now or later?"

"Now. In the morning, there are fewer people. Please, can I ask you to watch out for the young girl?"

"That one from yesterday?" One of the women smiled. "How old is this girl? You are such a modest guy."

"She's the daughter of a friend of mine."

"Oh? Then your friend is not just a friend; she is a young woman, not a child."

"That's enough of this nonsense. Would you be ready in about an hour?"

Adam sent Nata with a group of migrants to HIAS and finally calmed down. He had barely started work when an absolute wonder appeared in the hall. He looked like Charlie Chaplin, but he wore shoes of standard size. This cartoon character kept two little black dogs under his armpits. They were tiny but incredibly naughty; they squealed and barked. "Chaplin" lowered them onto a desktop, and they raced atrociously around, back and forth, showing their rat teeth. This hustler of dogs spoke with a heavy accent. "Is Betina here? Call her."

"No, she's not here, but she will be later. And you ... sorry, who are you?"

"I'm her husband. I'll wait for her here."

"Of course," Adam responded hastily. He squinted at the animals. "What cute doggies. By the way, I have been working here for a while, but I have not seen you."

"I do not interfere in my wife's affairs, and she doesn't interfere in my business. I go to auctions. I buy and sell paintings."

"Wow! Probably a profitable business?"

"I'm not complaining about my life."

He laughed, showing the same teeth as his dogs.

When Madam Betina got to the Zum Turken, the dogs became frantic. They shook on their tiny feet, screeching from excitement, and wanted the hostess to hold them. Adam thought the tiny dogs were about to suffocate from happiness.

"Chaplin" was not particularly welcome here, and the conversation was quiet at first but then got louder and louder.

He took his bowler hat, grabbed the animals, angrily slammed the door, and was gone.

Adam stood behind the counter and pretended he had not noticed the quarrel.

Madam Betina turned to him and spoke in a cold, dry voice, giving standard orders. Adam nodded respectfully, showing that he did not witness a family disagreement.

Madam Betina seemed to have appreciated his discretion; she already used a softer voice at the end of the speech.

"Adam, you have stayed for a long time in Austria. You must get a temporary residence permit. We must go to the government office to get that, where I will help you fill out all the papers."

"Thank you very much, Madam Betina."

She shrugged her shoulders—which communicated that it was not worth the gratitude—and she was gone.

While Adam and Kolya were working with new arrivals, Nata appeared around noon, accompanied by a nice-looking young man.

"Adam, this is Sasha."

"Hi." Adam squinted. "You look familiar. Have we already met, Sasha? Where do you live?"

"Of course, we met, Mr. Adam. You accepted me a few weeks ago. I live with my friends and family."

"Why didn't you go to Italy? Where are you going? What will you do?"

"So many questions." Sasha laughed. "I am a dentist. I want to go to Germany, to my friends."

"Adam, Sasha invited me to walk. I may come later in the evening," Nata said.

"Hmm, you're a big girl, and this a free country. But you should probably eat first. Can you sit down for lunch?"

"Don't worry. I will go with Nata into a café," promised Sasha.

"Well, good, fine. Nata, can you return by nine o'clock tonight? I'll be waiting for you at home."

"Thank you, Adam. I'll be home at nine."

Adam nodded and, when they left, turned to Kolya. "Did you see this type?"

"In my opinion, he looks like a nice guy."

"Something bothers me. Too many dentists are going to Germany to cure people's teeth. Why all of a sudden have dentists been knocked out of Russia? Why does Sasha intend to go to Germany?"

"Many doctors want to go to Germany. There they learn the language and get paid newcomers for six months," mentioned Kolya.

"I'll not be going to any country where people speak German. I can always hear words as they talk: *Halt, Achtung*."

"I agree. But it's all in the past, and now there are other people and other times."

"I understand this. But when I hear *Achtung*, I think Auschwitz."

"Adam, enough philosophy. New migrants came; let's go to work." Kolya waved his hands.

There were a lot of problems, but Adam could not relax. Ilya, who moved to Germany, had made him recall his hostility toward that country.

Where is Nata now with this lover of Germany?

Adam realized he was worried because of Nata.

Let her parents be worried about this.

But he worried in the evening, at home, waiting for her return. Time went by, and the girl still wasn't home.

Well, it is nothing. She will come. Where else can she go?
Adam looked at the empty street several times, but it was quiet. He returned to the dining room, feeling like a hen and blaming himself.
And why am I so nervous? Oh, anything could happen to her. But what can happen to a young girl in a strange city in the company of an elegant dentist? Even if she were my daughter—well, what could I do? Would I prohibit her from meeting with such a type? I could prevent it; I'm responsible for her. But why would she listen to me? I didn't listen to anyone at her age. But then I was a boy, and she is a girl.

When his patience had run out, Nata finally appeared.

"Thank you for coming!" Adam said sulkily. "I asked you not to be late. And where is your German dentist?"

"Oh, sorry, Adam, it is late. And Sasha, he's a good boy but a little dull. I did not ask him to visit us."

"Thank God. Now it is necessary to think of how to prepare for Italy. We have to find a decent family for you to stay with."

"And why do I need to stay with a strange family?"

"You don't understand. The waiting time for a visa to America takes half a year in Italy. So, you will need to pay for an apartment all this time, which is costly. All migrants are taken to Ostia or Ladispoli, the suburbs of Rome. You often will have to ride into HIAS, Rome, by train, for money and other matters, and there will be many. And I will not be able to help you in Italy. I'll be far away."

"Well, I'll settle down over there somehow. Thank you, Adam. I know you worried about me because you were asked to."

"I did help you get settled, yes? You're right; I was asked. But then I saw you—so young, naïve—and wanted to help you. That's why I worried so much."

"I know, Adam. Thanks for everything."

* * *

Before sending Nata to Italy, Adam cared for her as best he could all week. He treated her to some delicacies and arranged nice dinners in the evenings. Nata proved to be a real artist. She drew funny pictures, which often featured cats.

"In art school, people called me 'Kitten,'" she shared. "I studied drawing after school at the architectural college. My wish was to study art in America. When I was four, my drawings were exhibited in Japan. Imagine my parents' pride. They have friends in America, and they promised to help me first. Mom and Dad then decided to leave Russia. I'll get to the art college, study, and then do it professionally. They say that artists earn a lot of money in the United States. But my relatives want me to be happy."

"You have real talent. Everything will be fine." Adam smiled. *What's the use of destroying her illusions?*

He became attached to this lovely girl and worried, as a parent does, about seeing the child going away. Adam introduced Nata to a decent family, although who could know what was waiting tomorrow? The week passed quickly. When the time came for her to leave, Adam's soul was restless, and seeing her off was sad. The only encouraging point was that Nata promised to write.

Capital of Immigrants

Madam Betina, as promised, took Adam to receive a temporary Austrian passport. While riding in the car, they had a rare conversation: Madam Betina spoke about something other than work.

"You haven't changed your mind about the United States? What happiness do you seek in this America? What is it in your America? There you think the streets are paved with gold? Nothing is good there—no culture, the cities are dirty, and people are not well groomed. But Austria is the center of Europe. Here is beautiful architecture; it's a civilized country. Who will need you there? And now you'll get a *fremdempass*—a temporary passport. I can help you obtain Austrian citizenship. Work is what you lack. Live here, start a family, and enjoy life."

"Thank you, Madam Betina, but I wanted to see America long ago. Yes, and Igor is waiting for me there."

"Your friend, the doctor, I do understand. Think about what I said."

Registration for the fremdenpass went without incident. A nasty-looking man listened to Madam Betina, made Adam sign a statement paper, and took his photo. Madam Betina explained to Adam that the passport would be sent by mail.

They were already at the door of Zum Turken before she got on with her thoughts. She again tried to convince him. "Adam, think about what I told you. I think they don't need good people there, and you will be left out and be ignored."

Adam received a temporary Austrian passport in two weeks, showing it to everyone joyfully and pridefully. Other migrants, who had absolutely no documents, admired this passport. It was a mark of distinction.

Adam waited for his case and an interview at the US Consulate. He would be given a visa about a month later if he made a good impression. Days turned into weeks, and weeks into months.

* * *

Business at Zum Turken went on as usual. Traffic was heavy, but it had become habitual and brought some excellent earnings. Adam was already tired of Vienna. He wanted to move forward. His routine was sometimes interrupted by unexpected encounters. Once a plane arrived from Leningrad, Adam handled, as usual, the group of new migrants. Alex and Eugene, old friends of Adam's, were with their families. They had become friends while helping Adam's problems with sewer lines. The plumbing needed to be repaired, and there were some severe problems.

Adam, the manager of the big establishment, was responsible for everything and sometimes had to clean the pipes with a hunk of steel wire. Alex and Eugene worked as engineers in a company specializing in plumbing works. The historic meeting between the manager of the restaurant and the two engineers occurred at the restaurant's toilets. The guys were masters of such things and promised to help Adam fix the plumbing problems. It was solved, and they became good friends. They did together studied English outdoors. As it turned out, they also thought about leaving the country and they were going to learn a new language. They decided to study together. They even hired a teacher who traveled with them to nature and taught them a unique, fast-track modern system to learn English. These educational picnics ended up as often as all picnics did—vodka, good food, friendly company, and lots of joy and fun. Nevertheless, it was pleasurable for everyone.

Adam greeted his friends on arrival in Vienna and invited them to a party at his house. The conversations dragged on long after midnight; there were many questions. Adam described the long waiting time for American visas and the road to Italy. Alex and Eugene also intended to go to the United States, to Flint, a city near Detroit. They drank for New York and Detroit and meetings on American soil.

Another time, a group of migrants from Leningrad arrived. Among them was another friend, nicknamed Arny; his real name was Arnold. He had left Russia with his wife and grownup son. Their arrival in Austria was also celebrated at Adam's; as usual, they remembered the old days.

When he first met Arny, Adam had already moved to work in a commercial zone called Kupchino, where commercial enterprises constructed huge manufacturing factories. Those facilities are designed for hundreds and sometimes thousands of workers. Adam was in charge of feeding people working in these facilities. Adam met Arny, the chief mechanic, and they needed each other. Arny needed a food supply for his family. Adam needed help to fix his new apartment. Adam bought an apartment and needed electricians, carpenters, and plumbers, who were subordinate to Arnold. There was a huge problem with buying practically anything because of shortages in Russia. They were happy to meet each other.

They celebrated the meeting in Vienna with the usual Russian tradition: a good meal, vodka, and very long conversations.

Another surprise meeting happened during one of the dull days in Zum Turken: Caruso appeared in person with a large, seemingly empty suitcase.

"Balzac, hey!"

"Wow, Caruso! What kind of wind brought you here? I heard you were singing in Paris."

"I've just arrived from there. Did the rumor already spread that I got a job at the restaurant Rasputin?"

"Widely. Your success has swept across our migrant land. What are you doing in Vienna?"

"Balzac, I came to see you." He lowered his voice. "I need all the black caviar you have. I know the price and am ready to pay."

"Caviar, I do have, but I have a partner."

"I'll pay one hundred fifty schillings per jar."

"Caruso, you've always been a businessman. Come on, one hundred fifty-five, and it's all yours."

"Balzac, you've grown up; I'll pay one hundred fifty-five, but only if I get everything you've got."

"I have a lot. Tell me, how can you take so much across the border?"

"I'll sit on the train and get into Paris. Don't think about it, Balzac. It's my problem."

"Well, you're my hero, Caruso. Let's go. I'll show you the stock."

Caruso whacked Adam on the shoulder after payment was made for the goods. "Glad to see you, Balzac. Maybe we will meet another time. Be healthy."

He disappeared, and Adam long remembered their first encounter near HIAS.

After returning home, Adam counted the proceeds from that day and added that to the accumulated money from the past six months. It was a round sum, and he thought he had the right to treat himself with a gift. He had long dreamed about an elegant red velvet robe and lovely slippers.

The bourgeois dream quickly translated into reality, and Adam was pleased with his purchase.

Soon he received a call for a meeting at the American Consulate. His nerves went wobbly, particularly when he was in the office of the US consul. The consul was flipping through Adam's dossier and studying the details.

Finally, he asked, "Why did you leave Russia? You had a good job and made a good living. What is the reason for your departure?"

"I didn't want to stay in a country where a person has no rights, and nothing belongs to him. A job is not yours and can be taken from you tomorrow. The apartment is not yours; it can be lost. And your life is not yours. You can go to jail at any time just because someone decided to. Or, even scarier, there is generally no justice. It's just so. Do you understand?"

"Yes, well, thanks. You will receive a response within a month."

Adam walked away with mixed feelings. Had he made the right impression on the consul? Or was it in vain? Oh, he wished to know how it would all end in advance.

After a month, he got a call from the consulate with good news: his visa was ready. Mr. Adam Gardov was admitted to the United States with refugee status.

Adam clasped the phone with his palm, which was sweating. A short time ago, he had been a refugee in Austria without a certain future and had only a temporary passport. And now, he was a refugee with the prospect, in four years, of becoming a citizen of the most influential and prosperous country in the world.

Having obtained a visa, Adam went to Rav Tov. He was congratulated and told that he could leave Austria within two weeks. After that, Adam immediately arrived at the Zum Turken to tell Madam Betina the news, but it was already posted.

"It means you are still going? You had time to reconsider."

"Thank you, Madam Betina. I have made my decision."

"Well, as you know, I need to pick someone to take your place today or tomorrow. Please, work for one more week. Help the new person learn. And here's another thing, Adam." She looked at him intently. "You should see the attractions of Vienna. You have been working for six months without seeing the Vienna State Opera, Saint Stephen's Cathedral, or anything else."

"Of course, Madam Betina, I will see those." Adam looked confused. "And about the new worker—I appreciate everything and will take the time to teach someone."

* * *

Saint Stephen's Cathedral was considered a masterpiece and a symbol of Vienna. It was beautiful and majestic. Adam found it even grander, making an indelible impression on him. He experienced deep emotions while looking at the Opera House, which seemed to shine with its lights at night. Adam entered the box office, but his fever cooled when he saw the ticket prices. He did not enjoy the Austrian Habsburg emperor's residence as much.

It's all nice, but compared with the Hermitage in Saint Petersburg, it's not even comparable to their vast halls. The stairways there are majestic and splendid. And here is a small space; everything is somehow not royal. There isn't enough wealth.

He walked around Schönbrunn. He thought of riding horse carriages, but they were smelly. The Viennese Woods was the last place to visit on Adam's cultural program. It was rumored that Kafka and Freud loved walking here. While walking in the Viennese Woods, Freud always dreamed about something, which probably became the basis for his theory of psychoanalysis.

The month was May; everything was flowering, and it smelled magical. Adam strolled into the woods and hummed the melody from Strauss's waltz, "Tales from Vienna Woods," under his breath. He often heard it on Soviet radio as a tribute to the party and the cultural development of the Soviet people.

At the end of his tours, Adam climbed the observation tower and froze in awe as he looked at the open panorama and the spurs of the Alps.

On his day of departure, Adam arrived at the airport without a problem and passed inspection. He stepped aboard a US airliner, sat, and watched; his eyes didn't leave the window. His heart pounded strangely, agitatedly, and excitedly. It told him that he had finished another chapter of his life. He was ready to turn the page.

Arrival in New York

THE PLANE LANDED AT NEW YORK'S KENNEDY AIRPORT. Adam arrived and went to a vast hall that had many lines. He was sent to the line for immigrants. He presented his documents to the customs officer, but his Austrian passport was immediately returned. An officer studied Adam's visa carefully and intently stared at Adam. He was the only one of the arrivals who had emigrated from Vienna that day.

Now, I will be shamed. My visa will be revoked, and I'll be thrown back into Russia.

Adam was scared. The thought flashed in his head, but the customs official stamped a seal and said something Adam hoped was probably lovely. Adam translated this as permission to enter America.

He should have been met in the waiting room. There was a considerable crowd; people were waving signs with many names, and Adam tried to find his name among the abundance of bouquets, posters, and signs. Not seeing his name *Adam Gardov* he began to panic.

What if nobody picks me up? Where would I go? What should I do?

Capital of Immigrants

Adam noticed an old lady greeting newcomers on the line, holding a sign with his name. She spoke Russian with a clear accent, put him in a taxi, and paid for the ride. The old lady said goodbye to Adam and slipped him a note with an address. She told him not to forget to go to the office of Rav Tov. Adam was riding in the taxi, looking out the window. He enjoyed looking at the sign with his name written in English. From now on, he would be an immigrant.

The taxi delivered him straight to Brighton Beach. In this area of Brooklyn, many immigrants from the USSR had settled, mainly from a southern city called Odessa. But then, in the early 1980s, Brighton Beach did not resemble the future "Little Odessa."

The so-called hotel for Adam was paid for the week ahead. In a squalid room stood a narrow iron bed covered with soldiers' blankets and a bedside table—all of the furniture.

Adam sat on the bed and realized that he feared uncertainty, precisely how he had felt upon his arrival in Vienna. He went out of the room and down the hall. The window looked onto the filthy street. At the desk, a man was reading a newspaper in Russian.

"Sorry, can I make a call from here?"

"Only a short one. Here everything costs money. Where do you want to call?"

"It's here in New York City. I'll be quick; don't worry." Adam dialed the number.

"Hello, Igor? Hello! Yes, I flew in today. I am lodging at a hotel in Brighton Beach. Can we meet tomorrow? Where? Wait, I will write it down."

He covered the phone and asked the gloomy man, "Sorry, is it possible to get a pen and a scrap of paper?"

"Do you also need a key to my apartment?" He looked irritated and threw a pencil and a scrap of paper.

"Yep, Igor. Is Queens the street? Oh no, it's a borough. So, first, I ride to Forty-Second Street. Then I switch to the seventh train and ride to Jackson Heights, Seventy-Ninth Street? Yes, I understand. When I arrive, I'll have to wait outside at the stop and call you. Until tomorrow then."

Adam turned to the grumpy man. "Thank you very much for allowing me to call." The man growled, scowling.

* * *

The following day, Adam went to the lobby with his suitcase. An older woman was sitting at the reception desk.

"You're leaving us? So quickly? You don't like it here?"

"No, all is in order. Just going to meet my friends."

"That's good. To see friends is always a perfect idea."

"Tell me, please, how do I get to that address?"

"Sorry, I don't know. But the subway here goes not under the ground but on top. As you leave the hotel, turn right until you see the rails at the top. Ask some people there. There they all speak Russian."

Adam thanked the older woman and strode along the streets. There were dark shed-like houses, cardboard boxes, and debris everywhere.

Reaching a small café, Adam entered a semi-dark room and talked to the young fellow behind the counter. "Good morning! Coffee, please."

"Relax, countryman. You can speak Russian."

"Oh, cool. Can you tell me where the nearest Metro is?"

"But where are you going?"

Adam showed him a note with the address, and the guy shook his head.

"This is very far. First, you must ride to Manhattan and then train to Queens. Ask for a map directly from the cashier. They will give you a free subway map. For you, it's about two hours to ride, no less."

"Is that so far away?"

"See, you just arrived, huh?" the guy said, chuckling. "What will you do in the United States?"

"Realistically, I don't know yet. But in Russia, I was in the restaurant business. Here I want to do the same."

"Seriously?" The guy brightened. "Then buy my café."

"How would I buy this?"

"As a friend, I would give it to you for fifteen thousand."

"Dollars?"

"No, rubles. Come on, man; you're in America. I was recently burglarized, so I have to sell the business."

"Sorry, but I have no money."

The café owner immediately lost interest in Adam and only yawned at parting.

"You owe me fifty cents for coffee."

Adam put some change on the counter and quietly left.

Wow, $15,000! Where do people get this kind of money?

The Brighton Beach area would flourish thanks to a massive wave of new immigrants from Russia. There would be big shops and many restaurants, including Russian fast food, cafés, and bookstores. Vegetable and fruit stores would eventually be on every corner. There will be many clubs and bars that still have to be built. Ten years later, he could not foresee that such a place, a small coffee shop, would cost $100,000.

Adam saw a vast, tall, metal construction with strained wires high above, and the metro's rails looked very old.

Adam walked up the stairs to the cashier's booth.

He bought a token and asked the cashier for a map. When the rattling train arrived, he hurriedly entered inside. The doors closed, and the train went very fast at the altitude of the houses. It was damn scary; it seemed the wagon was about to crash or fly into the wall of the nearest house. Adam began to study the subway map, as this metro system was called in New York.

Many lines of all colors and shades were numbered or labeled with letters. They intersected and ran to all areas of the city. At first glance, everything seemed chaotic compared to the Leningrad (Saint Petersburg) and the Vienna subway. But upon closer look, Adam praised it, as everything was well thought out down to the last detail. During his first time in New York, he had taken an English map into his hands and could sort out where things were. He would now have unassisted access from one end of town to another.

What a map! Thanks, thoughtful people who created this map. Well done, guys. I've mastered English; once I decipher it, I can live here. This map does show Jackson Heights. And I think this is Queens. It's a borough, one of the five districts of greater New York. And every borough has its neighborhoods. Jackson Heights is one of them. Here is my stop. Okay, I have to get off there.

Capital of Immigrants

He called Igor from a payphone. After ten minutes, they met.

Talking about everything, they approached the house. All the way, Adam thought about Margo in the back of his mind. How to behave now? He was worried about how and what to say in such a delicate situation. Tingling tension also mingled with sincere, pure joy from meeting with Igor. They walked into the apartment, and the chill of excitement was gone. Adam gladly met Margo; her warm, hospitable smile melted the invisible, dangerous ice between them.

"Adam, how glad we are to see you! Wash your hands, and come to the table. It's all ready; we'll celebrate your arrival." Benny has been asking, 'When will Uncle Adam come?'"

"Hi, guys; I've also missed you all. Benny, look here. That is for you: a German locomotive. The rails are here, with all sorts of things for the railroad."

"Oh, Uncle Adam, thanks!"

His cheeks were rosy, delighted eyes glowed, and he sped away to play with the gift.

"Guys, this is for you—greetings from the Zum Turken."

Adam pulled out familiar standard migrants' sets.

"Here it is." Margo threw up her hands. "We missed black caviar and champagne so much."

"Igor, this is for you."

On the table appeared a big bottle of Stolichnaya vodka.

"We will drink after you pass the examinations."

"Thanks, buddy. Well, let's get to the table. Now we can get a shot of vodka; Tell us, Adam, how are Betina and the Zum Turken? Ilya called me someday from Germany. I didn't talk to him. He was calling collect."

"What is that?"

"When someone calls you, you have to pay for the call. Ilya lives on everything free and makes some money. But he calls me collect, knowing perfectly well every penny I have to count now. I must thank you very much for making me work last month. That helped us a lot. The money came in handy."

The evening ran its course. Adam's worries about Margo vanished; her behavior held no hint of the strange memories of their New Year's Eve story. Adam was overwhelmed by the delicious food, wine, and long-awaited friendly encounter. His soul was happy, and Adam felt so grateful for his luck that he almost shed a tear and had difficulty finding the right words to express his feelings.

"My dear friends, I love you so much. Behold. Whatever you want, I will do for you. So glad you are my best friends in the whole wide world. I don't even know how I would be here without you."

"With you, it's clear—no more drinks. You're a mess!" Igor laughed. "It seems that now is the right time to hit the sack. Margo put you in Benny's room. Get a good rest. Tomorrow we will go to seek an apartment for you."

The First Apartment

IN THE MORNING, Adam woke up with a terrible headache. *Why did I have so much to drink?*
In the kitchen, Igor sipped coffee and smirked at his sight.
"How is your head? Does it hurt?"
"Oh, God. About yesterday—I was drunk. I hope I said nothing stupid."
"Oh no. You only acknowledged your love for Margo."
Adam grew gray with fear.
"Just kidding; everything is okay. You already have turned green."
"Don't joke like that, please. I can't understand words with a hangover. My sense of humor is not working yet."
"Fine, let's have breakfast, and then we will look for a real-estate agency for your apartment. We must pay for the first and last months' rent, plus agency fees—100 percent of the monthly cost."
"It's necessary to pay three months of rent in advance? No break for a month or so?"
"It's the rule, brother. Do you have money?"
"Yes, I've saved $5,000. There was a lot of work lately, and Madam Betina tried to keep me there. She asked me to stay permanently and even promised help with citizenship."

"And you refused? I sometimes regret not having gone to Germany."

"What's for you in Germany? You are a Jew."

"I get tired of being a Jew. America, from afar, seems to be a paradise, and now when we are here, I'm thinking of scouting in Germany. If I like it, we will move back to Europe."

Adam could not say anything and almost said his thought aloud. *What about me?* But he bit his tongue in time and only frowned.

* * *

The real-estate agency was a ten-minute walk from Igor's house. Igor talked freely with the agent. Adam tried to guess what they were talking about. He had not particularly excelled at learning English in Vienna, but now he clearly did not understand this.

"Listen, Adam. They have a studio for rent here. The price is $195."

"What is it ... a studio?"

"A small apartment, a room combined with a kitchen. For one person, it's a good shelter; it even has a closet. It is all you need for now. Let's go and look at it."

Unfamiliar with such residential nuances, Adam was surprised that there was a hallway and the apartment only needed a table with chairs and a bed. There was a good bathroom, a cozy kitchenette, a gas cooker, and a refrigerator.

"I like it." He looked at his future residence. "The window looks weird, like the ones on Soviet trains that open a slide up and down but not to sides. Yet, there is this iron ladder outside the window."

"That is America. Everywhere there are fire-escape ladders at the window grate. The gate is locked inside, and only you will have the key. So, don't worry about thieves. You'll need only a bed or sofabed; the rest you can buy on Roosevelt Avenue. There are a bunch of stores. You choose everything you need; there is fast delivery. But first, drawing up a contract with the agency will be necessary—if you're satisfied with it, of course."

To Adam, it was suitable. He signed the rental papers, paid, got the keys, and said goodbye to Igor.

"Thank you. You lost half a day with me and must study now."

"Knock it off. If there are problems, call me. And congratulations on the new shelter. We are neighbors now."

Adam found a sofabed in one of the shops on Roosevelt Avenue; it was cheap, with a good mattress. The storeman promised to deliver it at seven o'clock that evening. Inspired by a successful transaction, Adam splurged more for a secondhand large color TV. The boy who worked in the store delivered it to the apartment and connected the antenna.

At the house's entrance, Adam stumbled upon a small nightstand.

Nothing used was sold here, and the tenants dragged things no longer useful in their homes to the trash. The building superintendent told Adam that Americans sometimes throw out good but no longer needed things. Adam cleaned it, and it looked almost like new. It fits perfectly under the TV set.

Finding a table and chairs would be lovely, but that's unlikely.

There was still time before evening, and Adam decided to return to Roosevelt Avenue to buy household utensils, dishes, and other stuff. Adam also wanted to buy good jeans and a jacket for a long time. This desire was his dream, like the red velvet robe, and he saw no reason to deny his longtime fantasies since he was in America.

Classic blue jeans his size wasn't available, but a velvet pair, also in a cowboy style, fit him perfectly. Adam looked in the mirror. There was a new American. He decided that now was the time to go to Igor and show off his fresh look, and at the same time, he would invite them to the housewarming party.

Margo opened the door. When she saw Adam, she threw up her hands and sobbed from laughter.

"What happened? Who's there?"

Igor followed her and couldn't hold in his laughter.

"What is so funny?" Adam was dumbfounded. "And I called you friends."

"You're a cowboy and need a hat and a pair of pistols, dude."

"Laugh, all you can laugh. My housewarming will be … let's do the day after tomorrow—Saturday evening. I'll prepare dinner. I have already planned salmon sandwiches, lettuce, egg, and tomatoes. There will also be a Russian herring with green onions and a nice oven-baked chicken."

"It will be the same as in Leningrad? When you treated us with the leg of lamb?" Igor was laughing.

Adam shook his head reproachfully, recalling the event. They had been drinking; the leg of lamb burned severely, and Igor frequently joked about this occasion.

"Of course, we will come," replied Margo. "Do you have chairs?"

"Come, everything will be ready. It's time for me to go. Some furniture should be delivered."

Capital of Immigrants

"Well done, man. You're settling in."

Delivery in New York worked perfectly; the sofa was at Adam's apartment at precisely seven o'clock. He noted with satisfaction that the room had gradually acquired a look of residential comfort. The mattress proved to be good. Everything made him happy—especially the cowboy costume.

Adam prepared his first homemade breakfast: oat cereal with dried fruits, tea, and toast with cheese. Eating with pleasure, he composed a list of what he needed to buy.

A pot, pan, and kettle. A table and four chairs. Dishes, glasses, cutlery. I also need a telephone. Everything else can wait. I must figure out how to get to Rav Tov. I need to find a job and learn about English courses. These things on the list shouldn't be a problem.

The utensils and furniture did not raise a problem; Roosevelt Avenue proved a paradise for shopping. But obtaining a phone was more challenging. Adam went into the store where they were on display and was asked for other documents regarding his apartment lease and an American visa. The clerk shook his head and explained something to him, stubbornly repeating, "Social Security card."

Some woman came out from the queue and spoke Russian. She explained to Adam, "You must register in the Social Security office. You need an identification number. You will be asked for it everywhere; you can't be without this card. It is as important as a passport."

"And where is it ... this office?"

"It's nearby. Write down the address. I'll explain how to get there."

Adam quickly found the office, but there was a long line to get a Social Security card. Adam joined the queue and was prepared to lose a half day, but soon he was called to a desk. He put all his available documents—his visa and temporary Austrian passport—in front of the woman filling out the paper.

"Russia?" Adam nodded.

She showed him a spot on the form and extended a pen.

"Sign here."

"What?"

She eagerly pointed to a line for him to sign on and gave him a card with numbers and his name.

Leaving the office, on the one hand, Adam rejoiced—he had solved the problem with the bureaucrats, and the correct paper could help him buy the phone. But on the other hand, he understood how urgently he needed to take English classes. Adam felt stupid not knowing how to answer questions. That irritated him when he couldn't understand what was being asked. He moved to learn the language up to the first spot on the list of essential things.

Adam connected the phone he had bought to the socket at home but didn't hear any signs of life. The clerk in the telephone shop had shown Adam four fingers, and he guessed what that meant all the way home. It looked like those magical four fingers were somehow associated with configuring the phone.

English Language Courses

ON SATURDAY, ADAM COVERED THE TABLE he'd bought and prepared the promised meal. He watched English-speaking TV and placed the whole chicken in the oven to brown.

When Igor's family came, the atmosphere in the apartment was homey. Here lived a man able to receive and love guests.

"Adam, you did great with all these furnishings. It's very cool." Igor paid tribute to the purity and beauty of the prepared table.

"But where is the leg of lamb?"

"Very funny." The master of the house rolled his eyes. "Will you tell the same joke forever? Will you blame me for that lamb to the end of my days?"

"Just kidding, kidding! I thought back to Leningrad and the good old times. Still, there was something glorious in those days. It was a simple life, but we didn't appreciate the joy."

"Oh, Igor, you're right, but now we are in America and should enjoy that life. By the way, do you know a good English school? I've had so many problems the past two days. With the telephone, something is not working; what is it? The guy in the store told me something, but I did not understand. He showed four fingers to me."

"The good thing is that it wasn't the middle one." Igor laughed. "The phone will be connected in four days. Margo and I often hear about the best English courses at the Cambridge Language Institute. The phone number is in the Yellow Pages. Well, are we going to sit at the table? Benny, wash your hands, and we will have dinner. Margo, tell him first about the meal and then the TV."

"Yes, but Adam has a big TV. The cartoons will look much better on the big screen. Adam, you have a huge screen. It's not like ours."

That compliment somehow made Adam feel awkward.

Dinner went on, and everything was nice and friendly. After a few toasts for the host and his culinary skills, Igor appealed to Adam.

"Now it's more important to pass our exams and start working, and then we'll buy big TVs," Igor said dryly. "For now, we have to decide where we will be. Adam, do you remember I told you I wanted to go to Germany? While I'm there, can you look after my family? Margo may need some help."

"That is not a problem. Have you already decided when you will go?"

"Yes, I'll go in one week." Adam couldn't believe his ears.

"So soon?"

"What's said has to be done." Igor looked at Adam carefully.

"Honestly? Igor, I did not expect you to set your sights on Germany seriously."

"In general, yes, I'm thinking about it. If it's okay, you could also move with us, Adam."

"Not to Germany. I don't want to learn the language or live there. Finding out that your new life in New York doesn't suit you is unexpected to me. I don't want to go with you. You're my best friend. But this is your life, and you do whatever you think is best for you and your family."

"We're both doctors. The conditions for private practice in Germany are much better than here. That's why we probably must move there. Margo, Benny has been watching TV for too long, and it's late already."

Adam understood. "I'll walk you guys home."

* * *

He returned alone on empty streets, and everything seemed hostile and weird.

Oh, wow, Germany! And this after so many years of talking about New York and America. He is not satisfied with America. I could have stayed in Vienna and gotten Austrian citizenship. I could not even succumb to temptation on New Year's Eve. Of course, this is not only due to Igor but still ...."

Those thoughts bothered Adam. Returning late in the night to his apartment, he felt almost physically that the relationship with Igor would no longer be the same. He couldn't help but have a sense of misguided expectations and disappointment.

* * *

On Monday morning, Adam went to find the Cambridge Language Institute for language courses.

The address was in Manhattan: 34 West Forty-Second Street. Adam did not understand what the word in that street address,

"West," meant, but he decided to go by subway to Forty-Second Street and sort it out.

Getting off the train, Adam found himself in the massive hall of Grand Central Station. Along with the flow of people, he made it out on the street and inadvertently froze. He stood in disbelief and watched an impressive view of tall skyscrapers on the streets. Crowds and endless streams of cars were frightening, and it seemed like they could crash into one another. No one noticed a strange pillar in the middle of the street. A sea of people flowed past him without even noticing.

So, this is Manhattan. I'm on Forty-Second Street.

He found building number 34 and pushed the heavy front door, focusing on the house number. In the big hall were two men in uniform behind the reception desk.

"May we help you?"

"Hi, it's you ... sorry, I don't speak good English." Adam showed them a piece of paper with the address. "What ... where ... I should be there ..." Guards explained something. Adam did not understand a word.

Finally, one of the men took him out on the street and, pointing further to the street, kept saying, "West, west. Understand?"

"No," Adam answered honestly. He was alone on the street, without understanding what to do next.

And what was it? West, West. Go there or what? For what? Is it the number 34 building? They don't want to let me get in? Maybe there is someone to ask?

Confused and still not understanding the new language, Adam went the way shown. Nervous and angry, he approached a number 2 East Forty-Second Street building.

Capital of Immigrants

And where to go now? As I understand it, the number of buildings is over, but the street continues.

He crossed the street, and on the first building from the corner, he saw a sign that read 2 West Forty-Second Street. *That must be the same, just inverted. It was the same street and number but divided into west and east. These Americans are pretty strange. Why is there such confusion? A poor imagination for street names?*

Although the more Adam thought about it, the more it made common sense.

The numbering on all streets was so organized; it was convenient; the city was divided into squares, east and west. When someone knew about it, finding an address couldn't be easier. If someone searched addresses in Russia, streets would be named after someone, for example, "Tankman Hrupitcky." Try to find that.

So, musing, Adam got to the building he needed and heard the familiar: "Can I help you?"

"Yes, you know, ah ..."

"Oh, Russia! Hold on."

The girl disappeared and returned with another young lady, who spoke in broken Russian. As it turned out, she was from Poland; she knew Russian as a foreign language but could explain something to Adam. It was all he needed to know. Three months' English classes cost $300. Classes will begin next week.

"*Neither zabutte (do not forget)*, Monday. At 9 a.m., *novi* (new) group," she warned.

Another week remained before the beginning of the courses, but Adam decided not to waste time and started studying English more seriously. He carefully watched debates on the TV; he could get, at best, two or three familiar words. He looked in the dictionary and watched TV, trying to understand what was going on, and it went better than in Vienna. But it still was confusing.

A few days later, Igor called.

"Where did you disappear? We were worried that you were sick."

"Oh no, I'm here. I enrolled in English courses. They will begin on Monday. In the meantime, I decided to study seriously."

"I understand. I'm leaving for Germany."

"For how long?"

"A couple of weeks. I want to go there to look around and talk to people. Listen, Alla came—remember her? She was with us on New Year's, remember? She will help you get to the Rav Tov to see the money-paid schedule for newcomers. Write down the number, call her, and then ask where you will meet. And don't forget about my family, okay? Look after Margo, or call."

"Of course. Don't worry."

Thoughts swirled around the departure of Igor and his firm intention to leave the United States. In his heart, Adam was bitter and sad. Deep down, Adam knew that it would be wise to stay home, and if he were needed, Margo would call. Adam called Alla, and they agreed to meet the next day.

Adam arrived at Grand Central Station in advance—the meeting place with Alla. With nothing better to do, he studied a map of the subway, which crossed all parts of the city except for Staten Island. The map showed where bridges led to that island.

Finally, Alla appeared provocatively dressed in a short skirt, a jacket that barely covered her large breasts and wearing oversized sunglasses. Adam immediately felt uncomfortable.

Capital of Immigrants

The New York office of Rav Tov was in a part of Queens called Williamsburg. They needed to use two connecting subway lines to get there, and Alla, not embarrassed by her appearance, walked ahead.

Williamsburg turned out to be not a very pleasant place. Everything around was cluttered, neglected, and very dirty. Everything was covered in graffiti: the short brick residential houses, offices, streetlamps, poles, sidewalks, and even the subway train they arrived in. A high wire fence surrounded the basketball courts. Some teens pounded the ball, shouting and cursing.

"Wow!" exclaimed Adam. "Who lives here?"

"Mostly religious Jews, men in black hats, wearing hairs with side curls. Also, many Latinos, people from South and Central America. A lot of illegal aliens. You'll see now."

They met men who wore black suits and black hats. The women were bundled up in long clothes that reached the ground, their heads covered with headscarves. Adam wasn't religious; most people from Russia weren't religious. For many years, all religion was prohibited in that country. And now he saw all these people walking free, doing what they believed in and dressing as they wished. It was a new and strange feeling.

* * *

The Rav Tov office was crowded. A large group moved and talked at the same time. It turned out that many who came in for the first time could not receive their allowance. A resentful man punched a wooden wall, breaking it in the end. The crowd was militant and did not want to wait one more minute. Finally, the cashbox opened, and immigrants began receiving allowances.

When Adam got to the cashier, he searched for his name for a long time and was eventually issued $300. Alla merely snorted. Adam was delighted with this outcome and happy to get out of there.

"Adam, that's it for such office. In HIAS, people get a regular allowance six months after their arrival. In this joint, heaven forbid, there are benefits for only three months."

"Look, they could give us nothing," Adam expressed. "I thank them for whatever I get."

They went to the subway. Adam thought Alla would be expecting him to ask for another meeting. He did not say anything. She paused and said, "Well, if you need anything, call me. You have my number."

"So far, I'm good. Thanks for the help."

Adam didn't have any intention of phoning Alla. Back then, neither he nor she knew where they would be in a few months. He often remembered Nata, and not knowing where she was now brought him sadness and regret. She had promised to write a letter. Maybe she could write him, but where would she send it? Keeping the promise was almost impossible.

* * *

The long-awaited Monday came, and Adam started English classes. The classroom was noisy; all spoke different languages, and Adam met with some Russian people. The teacher was a pleasant, lively, energetic young man. His only downside was that he refused to speak any language but English.

"No, my friends, no," he said patiently with a smile when he rejected Adam's attempt to explain that his level of knowledge was zero.
"No Russian, only English. Just English, understand? I'm your teacher. You are students. How do you do?"
"Nice to meet you."
He shook Adam's hand. He had such a sweet face, showing the joy of meeting that it was impossible not to understand.

* * *

From the very first lesson, everything was exclusively in English. During a break between lectures and conversations, people talked about the teaching method in this school. Many knew this system, but Adam did not belong to that group.

Well, at least a little Russian would be helpful, so I could minimally understand here.

His group had three people from the USSR, one from Japan, one from Iran, and another bunch of people from God only knows where. Everything was challenging; however, no one had promised it would be easy.

Adam was in despair after the first day of classes and wanted to change courses. But then he pulled himself together and decided now that he had undertaken this, he must continue until he had completed the course. Moreover, the $300 paid for the courses could not be returned. He looked during the lectures at the calm, polite Japanese student and realized that it was even more difficult for him. For example, when he needed to say the simple phrase "I have," the Japanese student turned red, wildly tried, and cried aloud in a guttural voice, *"I hab!"*

Adam mentally commiserated with him.

The poor devils. Their throats are arranged differently, and I complain that I struggle to learn.

Oddly enough, the technique of total immersion brought its fruits. Little by little, Adam started to communicate, and he could carry on conversations with shopkeepers and cashiers in the subway. And when watching TV, he could distinguish between individual phrases and even grasp the context.

One day the phone rang.

"Oh, Igor, hi. Are you back from Germany?"

"Yes, already. Adam, what happened? You never even called Margo; she's upset with you."

"I'm sorry. You must excuse me. I had courses and classes and have been looking for work. I thought if Margo needed me, she would call. Did you like it? Are you moving to Germany?"

"Not yet. We will take exams here. Well, we have to do it."

Adam hung up with a heavy feeling. He felt guilty that he didn't call, but on the other hand, she could call herself to ask how he was doing. It seemed that here was the end of the friendship.

Yes, and Igor himself first started. Who was to blame for the friendship suddenly getting sour?

The reasons for it were not from Adam's side. Maybe it was Germany; Igor ultimately was ready to move. It was bitter and annoying.

The English classes began well, but things went downhill as soon as one month had passed and another teacher arrived.

It turned out that the school rules were that the teacher changed each month, so students must understand different voices, speech, and communication. Adam was discouraged and cried aloud, "God, I've only learned a bit! And now they have given us more problems."

Imperceptibly and discreetly, three months flew by. The course ended, and even the Japanese student had started speaking a little better by not throwing out words from the throat. Adam could have moved on to the next level and learned the language better, but the money was no longer flowing. The Rav Tov's help had ended. Adam must look for a job.

He knew that his former position as a restaurant general manager in Leningrad was irrelevant in America. He would have to build a career from scratch, competing with younger people, but he already had much experience. He would have a good chance if he could be fluent in English.

He had to think about finding ways to open his own business—and, most importantly, what kind? It would be understandable that it should be linked to the food-preparation industry. He had worked all his life in that area. But what would he do exactly? Restaurants were costly projects; financially, it couldn't be done now. He then learned an unfamiliar word, "franchising." It turned out that some big companies sold rights to conduct business. The company would help one find a location, teach, help pick up staff, and perform other miscellaneous duties. But franchising was very expensive and complicated. To run the business, franchisees must buy the name, license, products, and everything else. Also, it required a diploma of higher education in this field and several years of management experience in the

American market. That was also an issue. Adam noticed that all institutions related to food were called restaurants. Genuinely chic, ordinary eateries, coffee shops, and small restaurants are all called restaurants. Staff in such establishments worked from morning until night, and earnings were small. One must work around the clock to earn decent money at coffee shops.

Adam had only a pair of hands and a bit of savings, which, by the way, was melting away. No, this business was not for him.

What business could he start for a small amount of money without hiring labor? If he could start alone, he could handle the taxes, business expenses, and everything else. It was time to survey the field for the fight; he would look for work in a fast-food business. He would get into it and see how it works. And from there, with God's help, he would see where the path would lead.

Adam bought newspapers and looked at the employment announcements. The English courses had taught students that one couldn't just come in off the street to work. It was necessary first to call and arrange a meeting, an interview. Students also were told that any delay from the appointed time was unacceptable. A résumé must be prepared.

* * *

Adam chose the most attractive ad from the newspaper, and it was a miracle. He was invited for an interview in the office of Burger King the next day. Three minutes before the appointment, he entered the office and was sent to a room where a man sat. He was slightly older than Adam.

"Hello, my name is Joe Sanders. Adam, I looked up your résumé and want to ask, what position are you seeking?"

"Excuse me, Mr. Sanders—"

"You can call me Joe."

"Thank you, Joe. I do not pretend to be in any high position. I am ready to start from the lowest level."

"Adam, you have good English and worked as a large restaurant's general manager. How would you adapt to a position of junior assistant?"

"I have no ambitions as of today. I want to learn how the business operates, like everyone else."

"It's not very good to have a lack of ambition. That means a person does not want to grow in the profession."

"I'm not saying that I do not want to grow. Right now, I'm ready to take any work."

Adam returned home in high spirits. He had acquitted himself well in the interview and had gotten a job. He was accepted as assistant manager with a probation period of two weeks.

* * *

He could be promoted if he did well at work.

Adam was noticeably happy. He had to go to his first job in New York City early in the morning. It was time to grab the opportunity. Employees usually get in through the service entrance of the fast-food restaurant Burger King. They were boys and girls, barely older than fifteen years. The first manager turned out to be much younger than Adam. He told Adam to look around and get acquainted with the situation. That was what

Adam needed—to look around. He considered each room. There were large refrigerators and freezers. He studied the equipment and watched how they completed the preparation work. An hour later, the general manager appeared. He barely glanced at Adam and advised him to take a while to get familiar. Adam felt he was not so welcome here against the backdrop of nimble workers. To the youngsters, he must seem old.

Soon, all were occupied by work. There were ten cashiers, two assistants for each one, and the kitchen crew. All took their positions, and the restaurant opened. As if by magic, everything went into motion at the exact moment. Many people lined up immediately in front of each cashier, and orders flew through the kitchen: grilled burgers, or, as they are called here, Whoppers. All were quickly wrapped up, sent to the microwave for a few seconds, and then passed into an area of the counter with particular kinds of metal sections separated for each product. Thin slices of frozen potatoes called french fries were fried in oil. Whoppers were stacked on sliced buns, and people added mayonnaise or ketchup, lettuce, tomato, and cheese. Sodas or milkshakes accompanied most of the orders.

The crew smiled constantly. The stream of visitors was stunning, but not one of the attendants fussed or panicked. The process had been perfected, run like an ideal mechanism, and Adam was utterly unneeded. Later he asked how much time processing one order took, and the manager told him that a good cashier must take an order, get money, and serve the customer with the order in thirty seconds.

This Burger King restaurant ran at this crazy pace for a few hours and then got quiet. The manager sent some of the workers home. Those workers did not willingly punch their cards at the clock. Adam noticed that the general manager amended the punched cards with marks. He crossed out the extra minutes and corrected them all to four hours.

Noticing Adam's look, the manager explained that these staff members were not yet sixteen years old and, by law, must not work more than four hours. He closed the topic, offering, "Adam, you can have lunch. Try the chicken sandwich and fries. Enjoy it. Have fun."

Adam saw the junior manager chatting quietly about something with the general manager in the middle of the day. Then a junior manager disappeared into the storage room, came out with a large package, and handed it to the boss. Then Adam saw a stranger at the back door accept the goods. Some money changed hands, and the person left.

Here's the answer to why they do not want me here. All Americans eat that food daily, and there are probably regulations for product damage or some percentage of natural loss. I wonder how they cover the loss. And what here can they sell quickly? The same Whoppers and filets?

Late at night, returning home, he thought that rogues and tricksters existed everywhere. Adam wouldn't rat on them but learned the lesson for the future. After one day at Burger King, he felt he had been on the wrong side of this business and no longer wanted to be in it. He barely finished the three mandatory days and said goodbye to his former comrades on the fourth. Nobody asked him why; they didn't care. He was told to wait through the week and expect mail with the check with his earned money.

Adam again looked at the newspapers and found an agency specializing in restaurant employment.

* * *

He wasn't asked many questions at the agency that conducted the interview.

"Is this the first time you are here? We have a cashier job vacancy."

"I never did cashier work."

"And what is there to know? You'd be a cashier. The salary is $225 a week. Our services are equal to the salary for the first week. We return the money if you and the employer do not get along like old friends after one week. Everything is simple."

Adam counted out the required amount, received a piece of paper with the restaurant's address Roma di Notte, and went there. The owner was on-site and immediately asked a bunch of questions. Adam answered quickly, clearly, and correctly.

"Well, Adam, come tomorrow at ten in the morning. Wear a black jacket, white shirt, and bow tie."

Adam was walking home and could not believe he had maintained the conversation in English. It was amazing how smoothly he had passed the interview. Yes, the money for the language express courses was well spent.

Roma Di Notte

BEING AN IMMIGRANT IS PRIMARILY MEANT TO BREAK OLD TIES, start from scratch, learn a new language, and adapt to a new lifestyle, friends, customs, and norms. Generally, new arrivals had children and elderly parents. Another was added to all adaptation problems: constant responsibility for those who depended on you and constant fear that you would fail.

Immigrants had nothing. All the goods and meager belongings brought with them were unnecessary. Electrical goods were not suitable for the local outlets, clothes were not suitable for the local weather, and life values were not suited to the local mentality. They had to acquire things and experiences all over again.

Adam did not have half of these problems, but questions arose daily. The main thing now was to find a good job. Adam had never worked as a cashier. He prayed to God that he and the boss of Roma di Notte would like each other. However, he quickly realized it was just the beginning.

Roma di Notte was a typical Italian restaurant. At the entrance, guests met a giant sculpture of Caesar. There was a restaurant, a bar, and a nightclub downstairs in the building that belonged to the owner. The design of the nightclub, located in the basement, was in the form of caves, and dark lighting gave it comfort and intimacy in the evening. At the side of the dance floor, a live quartet played. Everything was very colorful. On Fridays and Saturdays, the club was always entirely occupied.

Adam's work was to take care of payments and check credibility with the bank over the phone, despite the wild noise of the band and noise from interacting visitors. In those times, in the 1980s, there were no scanners, automated teller machines, or contacts on credit cards. He could not even imagine electronic bank cards and simple procedures in his dreams. And Adam had to work with all of it for the first time.

A waiter came with a credit card, and the guest check and threw it to Adam.

"Come on—quickly, man."

"What do I do with this?"

Adam held in his hands, for the first time in his life, a banking credit card. And it was someone else's.

"Call the credit company, ask for the approval code, and fill in the form."

"Is this a joke? With my English? Where do I call, what do I ask, and what is their phone number? Is there anyone I can ask?"

"I don't have a clue. That is your job, man."

Oh, yes! They loved the word "man": "Hey, man! How are you, man?" But this supposedly friendly familiarity meant nothing. No one wondered how you were. All of them spit, "It's your problem, man."

Capital of Immigrants

There was pure truth. It was only his problem. Adam had never dealt with credit companies; he could not imagine how to do it and with whom to talk. In the middle of the restaurant were explosions of laughter and music. He managed to hear someone's voice; a poorly audible voice said something on the phone. How strange! He heard and understood someone who dictated this damn approval code to him. Adam entered the numbers into the form of payment. The waiter sped away with the check to the customer and soon brought Adam a copy of it.

"If you lose it, prepare to pay some bucks."

"I'm not going to lose it. I will even take it to the toilet with me."

"What toilet? Forget it." The waiter chuckled. "Hold the next account. Come on, Russian, work."

Adam was already used to immigrants from the USSR, regardless of nationality, being called Russians. If you spoke Russian, it meant you were Russian.

The phone rang. Adam picked up the phone, and he heard someone babbling without stopping. He heard English words. But he did not understand a single word. Someone asked, "Yes?" Adam, in fear, answered, "No," and hung up. Immediately the boss came over. "Why did you say no?"

Adam was scared. *God, he is going to fire me. I am gone.*

"I...I messed up."

"You're in America and not in the Soviet Union. Here we can't say no to a customer."

Soon the phone rang again. The boss stood nearby. Adam heard the intermittent voice mumbling and cheerfully said, "Yes."

"What is that? Why did you tell the customer we have the osso bucco ready now?"

"You told me that I couldn't say no."

"Yes, but the osso bucco needs an hour of preparation time. If you say yes, customers will think it is ready now."

The boss looked at Adam. He thought he would be fired tonight.

* * *

He collected the revenue at midnight and waited to be checked, afraid of being fired. But the boss just wearily said, "Tomorrow at ten. Don't be late."

A week passed, and Adam still worked at Roma di Notte. He had learned to call Visa, American Express, and Mastercard.

After a few days, everyone seemed to be talking about a strike. Adam didn't understand what it was about and paid no attention until asked.

"Russian, where do you live?"

"In Queens."

"But, tomorrow, how will you get to work?"

"Like today. By subway."

"You what? Do you not know that the strike begins tomorrow? The subway will not work."

Adam finally made sense of the debate he'd heard about the strike.

"Come by car, Russian. Just know that there can't be fewer than two people. An order from the mayor is that cars with one person are not allowed during a strike in Manhattan."

Capital of Immigrants

"But I have no car."

"This is your problem, man."

Adam worked in a first-class restaurant and was required to have the proper attire. He figured it would be about three hours walking from home to work. At six, no later, he would have to get up to be in place by ten. The plan was simple and good, but he did not consider one thing—Adam had only one pair of shoes unsuited for long hikes. These were beautiful shoes, bought especially for his working uniform.

He got to Roma di Notte by ten, but he had injured his feet with bloody blisters. His boss praised him: "Well done; you're not late. If you want to work here, always come on time."

Late that night, exhausted, Adam walked home, cursing the strikers, the manufacturers of those accursed shoes, the boss, and—he was scared to say—even America.

He walked on streets of darkness and horror. Sometimes a dog ran out and barked.

Thank God that was not a person. Dogs only bark. Who lives in this area? The poor, street gangsters, and illegal aliens. There is only fear.

He got home at three in the morning, and at six in the morning, he was on his feet again. They ached, and he whined about not having rest. He could barely pull his only pair of shoes onto his swollen feet. Moaning and groaning, he went to earn a second pair, dreaming of buying some soft, light shoes. It was evident that walking for three hours to the restaurant would be challenging, but he continued. He had to do it to satisfy his boss. Suddenly he heard the loud noise of squeaking brakes. A young guy was sitting behind the wheel.

"Hey, man! Going to Manhattan? Jump in."

"I don't have the money for a ride."

"I don't need your money. One person in the car is not allowed in Manhattan."

That is a good point. It means the fellow is not a Good Samaritan. He just needed a companion.

The first thing at work, Adam asked the barman, "Gino, where can I buy good shoes?"

"You need sneakers. Let's go."

"I thought 'sneakers' was a chocolate bar."

Adam tried on sneakers in the store and felt that these shoes were masterpieces. He was overjoyed and told the salesman, "Do not pack them up. I will put them on."

Gino, the bartender, was short in stature but heavy. He was very good-natured. He worked in the dining room upstairs and became the first person with whom Adam made friends in New York. Adam sat behind the cash register upstairs in the daytime near the bar. Gino read newspapers and sometimes talked with Adam on various topics. He spoke about the restaurant business and the host of Roma di Notte.

From Gino, Adam learned many things about the restaurant business in America. Firstly about the restaurant team and service. The waiter was the one who waited on customers and served them. The busboy had a lower-ranking post; he helped the waiter, took dirty dishes, brought fresh tablecloths, etc. The captain was a step above the waiter. He was responsible for everything that happened in the halls and the kitchen and was considered the main person in the restaurant. He took orders, accompanied visitors to the tables, and always had to be in the dining room if customers needed anything. The highest level was maître d'hôtel, maître d' for short.

"Our boss is lucky," said Gino. "That building was once the town morgue. So, he got a lease on it for forty-nine years. It's the same as owning the property. It's a four-story building in the heart of the city, understands? That is very prestigious. Although the restaurant does not bring him much money, it does not matter because he leases the rest of the building."

"Indeed, he is lucky. But why is there such a small income?"

"Earlier, it was a high-class Italian restaurant. Our delightful place was quite popular. And now Roma di Notte has no business. The kitchen here is not so good. Most of the customers are not happy with it. Besides, the boss himself works as a captain. His task is walking around the dining room, greeting regulars, smiling, and sometimes joking or nodding to a friend. However, he rushes in here with orders as in the role of a captain. It's very unprofessional, and people feel uncomfortable."

"Gino, you know so much about this business. I am learning a lot from you. And the more I learn, the less I want to be a cashier. The boss promised to increase my pay if I help in the coat check room."

"Yes, there is also trouble with the coat check. Customers come into the upper dining room, but there are not many. But it can't be closed because people need the coat check room. Before, when the restaurant was busy, the boss could rent to someone the coat check room for $5,000 a season."

"Wow! That's a lot of money. He wouldn't need to pay a salary; he could make money from renting space. Now it is summertime, and he could close this coat check room."

"It's impossible. The prestige could fall. Let's say someone came in with a hat. What to do with it? When customers see this, they think it is wrong; they don't like it."

"Yes, Gino, I understand that. Sometimes I could replace the girl who should work in the coat check and get a dollar from each coat or hat. But I'd rather be a bartender like you. Can you recommend any courses to me?"

"Buy a bartender book. All the recipes are there. Read and learn. And I'll show you in practice how to make cocktails."

Adam's additional earnings in the coat check room were little, but it increased his cashier wages. Adam worked in the dining room six days a week and received six to ten dollars daily as a coat check attendant. In addition, three times a week at night, he worked downstairs in the nightclub. It was absolute hell. Adam wanted to get up to the next level and find work as a bartender. And this possibility presented itself to him faster than he could have expected.

Gino suddenly died. Adam was stunned by this. And it was even more unpleasant when the boss got behind the bar, replacing the bartender. Adam understood that the boss should withhold such a duty and offer himself for the role.

"I can do the cashier job and be the barman. Gino has taught me some."

The boss didn't like that idea, but Adam had already decided to look for another job if he refused. The boss was not going to contribute to his promotion.

So, Adam again went to a recruitment agency and asked them to find him a job as a bartender.

"We have requested the bartender position from a restaurant called Orsini's. That is an excellent restaurant. Is it suitable for you? It's $250."

**

Signor Orsini was a tall, skinny, middle-aged Italian man with a long bird nose. He said the previous bartender had died, so they looked for a new one.

What misfortune attacked the profession? Adam was stunned.

He replied aloud that he did not have enough experience, but he had a lot of desire to learn and could quickly master the complexity of bartender work.

"Where did you work?"

"I'm working at Roma di Notte for one more week; then I'm leaving."

"Oh, that's Andreo's place." Signor Orsini nodded. "Your boss is my longtime competitor. Why do you want to leave there?"

"I do not want to be a cashier. In addition, there is little work, and I am getting bored."

Signor Orsini liked this response. "Well, Adam, be here in a week."

Orsini's

UNEXPECTEDLY, IT SEEMED THAT FORTUNE was finding Adam's lost connections. First, he heard from his sister, Sonya, by phone. She was older than him. She always loved giving advice and left for the United States a year before Adam. That was when he had advised her to emigrate, and she had listened to him on this rare occasion. In Leningrad, she had been an unmarried woman with a child, working in hazardous occupations and living in a communal apartment. Life in the USSR provided Sonya only with tangled darkness and suffering. They had never been close, but they began to get along after the death of their mother. When Sonya left with her child, the connection was lost. Adam had not received any news. And suddenly there was a phone call.

"Hello, how are you? Remember me?"

"Sonya, how did you find me? Where are you now?"

"The Jewish agency told me you immigrated to New York. I'm in Washington."

"And how is it there?"

"Well, John and I live in a high-crime area. Mostly, those who live here get by on a special program called 'welfare.'"

"Can you come here, and we'll discuss everything? Maybe you'd better move to New York."

"Adam, I'm thinking about it. I'll call you to meet me there. If I decide to, can you help us settle?"

"Of course. Don't worry about it. Call me."

A few days later, Adam found Nata's letter in the mailbox. His heart pounded faster, and an involuntary smile appeared on his lips. That was a delightful surprise. How did she find him? Nata wrote that she lives with her parents' friends on Long Island, a suburb of New York. She was going to attend drawing classes at the architectural institute. Her mom and dad had been denied permission to emigrate, and they had all grieved. She had obtained Adam's address from Igor through her parents' friends, and she asked Adam to write her with his home phone number. Then she could call, and they could meet. Adam was so delighted by the news that he called Igor to share this story.

"Hopefully, you're not going to meet with her, Adam. And keep in mind that if you will fool around with her, our friendship ends. Her parents are relatives of my good friends, and I don't want to be responsible for this girl."

After this conversation, Adam felt angry about all of it.

What rights has Igor to talk to me like that? Our friendship is already over. He was the one who wanted to go to live in Germany.

Adam wasn't planning to start a relationship with Nata, but who would dare stop him? It was nobody's business. Because of this nonsense, he wrote a polite letter to Nata and included his phone number.

Orsini's Restaurant was very different from Roma di Notte's. It occupied two floors. The Italian food and service were top-notch, and everything was of the highest class. A cute, black-haired Italian maître d', Nino, showed Adam his workplace—the bar on the second floor. The dining room was spacious and bright; a few people had already prepared tables for lunch.

"Guys, this is Adam, our new bartender," Nino presented him. "He's new, so go easy on him. Help him when he needs it." He added a few words in Italian, and everyone laughed.

"Issidoro, Mario, come here. Adam, these are our captains. For all questions, refer to them."

Both men shook Adam's hand. Issidoro told Adam what to do.

"Look, here is the alcohol. You put checks here. Have you worked with checks?" Adam nodded.

"Fine. Check everything out and learn the bar menu. Soon the business lunch starts. It is usually a lot of work."

Adam glanced into the dining room. Some of the service guys wore brown jackets, and some were white.

"In the brown are waiters, and in the white are busboys, right?"

"Well done. You understand," Issidoro praised him. "You'll get used to it."

Yes, thanks to Gino for his lessons.

One of the waiters approached Adam. "Hi, my name is Yugoslavo. I'm from Yugoslavia."

"Adam, from Russia."

"That means you will be called Russian."

"I know. I was called such in Roma di Notte."

"You did not get upset?"

"No, I got used to it."

"Good! Let's go. I'll show you how to prepare a cooler for the white wine."

They entered the back room adjacent to the bar. Yugoslavo poured a gallon bottle of white wine into a large flask and explained, "Adam, at lunchtime, we serve white wine by carafes. That's the cooler for wine. Remember that the big carafe is a whole, and the little carafe is half. We write all on the checks. You must put the prices onto the checks. Issidoro and Mario will help you. Here's Issidoro, the main man."

"And who is Nino?"

"Nino is the maître d', but Issidoro, though he is just a captain, is Orsini's relative. We have fifteen minutes before the rush. Keep that in mind. Let's go into the kitchen for coffee."

"*Ragazzi*, (boys), this is our new bartender."

That was addressed to the cooks, but all four were very busy in the kitchen, and there was no time for Adam.

"Okay, after lunch, you will be introduced. We should leave cooks alone for now," explained Yugoslavo. He handed Adam a cup of coffee and a cheese sandwich.

They ate a little and returned to the dining room. Issidoro appeared with a bundle of checks and a sheet of paper.

"Adam, keep the checks. Others listen. All tables got rearranged for today's lunch. We will serve following the number of orders. Let's go! The first table has four people; table number two has three people ...."

Waiters and busboys ran back and forth with cutlery and napkins, covering tables, and Adam could barely keep up with the events. Nino met customers downstairs, noted them in his list of bookings, and walked them to the stairs. Upstairs, they were greeted by one of the captains, Issidoro or Mario, and invited customers to their tables. Waiters helped them sit; they pushed and moved chairs and asked what they wished to drink. Now the busboys poured glasses of cold water with ice. The customers were left alone for a few minutes, and soon the seventy people had already thumbed through the lunch menu. They drank water and dipped warm breadsticks into olive oil while talking loudly.

Waiters rushed to the back room, poured white wine, wrote on checks, and quickly ran away.
"Russian, a glass of red."
"Which one?"
The waiter himself grabbed a glass, poured, and recorded it.
"A bottle of Santa Margherita, blanco! Fast!" That was Issidoro.
"Where is it?"
"Ah!" He ran to the refrigerator for wine.
"Russian, whiskey sour on the rocks."
Oh, I know that.
A delighted Adam began to mix whiskey, lemon juice, and ice cubes in a shaker. Then he poured the mixture into a wide whiskey glass and squeezed a slice of the lemon peel onto it.
"Come on, come on, faster." He was hastened from all sides.
"Table six—orange juice."
"What do I serve that in?" "Highball."
Adam leaped into the back room to squeeze fresh orange juice.
A highball—it's like a tall, narrow glass.

Capital of Immigrants

He quickly poured the juice.

"Russian, are you done? Write two dollars on table six."

After that, the orders for drinks came even faster. The orders for food began to arrive. Captains drew orders on notepads. The first copy went to the kitchen, and the second went to Adam. He had to rewrite their doodles in typographic check forms onto the corresponding numbers of the tables and place them into the appropriate check slots.

From the kitchen came the first orders, and Adam watched as the show began. In the dining room were serving carts on casters. On each stood two little gas stoves. A kitchen waiter brought in different pans with lids and warm table plates. The captain put pans on burners and moved the cart to the table, and the customers saw everything prepared right in front of their eyes.

Now hot appetizers were served, as they were called here. The appetizer was usually a pasta split for two, prepared masterfully in Orsini's. The pasta was cooked al dente.

A decent piece of butter, pasta, salt, and freshly ground pepper went into a pan. The pasta was twisted and placed onto warm plates in two equal portions. On the next stove was the warm sauce.

Parmesan was grated generously, and there were graceful movements with a fork and spoon.

On top of this went sauce and then grated parmesan, and it was served to the customers with the inevitable *"Bon appétit."*

Once the appetizer was finished, the show's second course kicked off. A kitchen waiter brought new pans with lids. Dishes were heated over a fire and then presented on hot plates. They were garnished with fresh sautéed broccoli in garlic sauce, fresh green peas, and carrots, thinly sliced and cooked with butter. To finish, veal in wine sauce with lemon went on the plate along with garnish, and a work of culinary art called *veal piccata* was placed in front of delighted customers. Sometimes customers ordered something else from the menu, but most preferred traditional, familiar dishes.

Lunch concluded with a cup of coffee or a cappuccino with a piece of cake. The most popular was called chocolate mousse cake, and the second had a strange name—*Zuppa Inglese* ("English soup")—and both were great. But Adam, once he had tasted the chocolate mousse cake, decided that he had never eaten anything better in his life.

The end of Adam's lunch turned into a stressful moment. He had to close all accounts and issue checks simultaneously. Issidoro and Mario came to the bar with Adam; they counted and filled in all the checks. Waiters carried them to the tables and immediately returned them with credit cards. Each card was processed, and forms were generated. Adam had to call the credit card companies for the confirmation codes. After a customer signed a check and indicated a tip, the top part went to Adam, and the customer kept a copy.

While captains said goodbyes and exchanged pleasantries with guests, Adam checked to see everything was in order: whether the check was signed correctly, the correct copy was left, and the total amount was correct. When the last customer left the restaurant, all started to talk loudly.

"*Ragazzi, ragazzi*, did you see this guy on table six? The girl ordered four glasses of orange juice! I thought the guy wanted to punch her."

"The juice is not champagne. Remember when the famous Russian ballet dancer Nureyev came? Ten times he ordered a glass of champagne. I told him, 'You can order a nice bottle of champagne,' and he said, 'No, I like it by the glass.'"

"And what do you care?" Adam was surprised.

"We sell cheap champagne by the glass," explained Issidoro. "If the customer does not specify what brand he wants and asks, for example, for a glass of wine or a whiskey, we pour out house stuff. It's a cheaper grade of alcohol but is sold for the same amount. And this Nureyev, with ten glasses of champagne, could be charged the same amount as if he had had a bottle of Dom Perignon."

"And how much does this bottle of champagne cost?"

"Five hundred dollars."

"Good Lord!"

"I know? Okay, people, lunchtime." Issidoro strolled into the kitchen.

Adam noticed that guys began to chuckle behind Issidoro's back. Adam carefully whispered and asked Yugoslavo, "Why do they laugh?"

"That is our captain's weakness," he grinned. "He loves Dom Perignon champagne. When someone orders a bottle, Issidoro always pours a glass for himself. He can't help it. Yes, you'll see it soon. Believe me, the evening performance will begin more abruptly than the lunchtime show. Let's go to the kitchen and get a meal there."

All gathered in the kitchen, and one of the waiters told Adam, "Hey, the new man. Yes, you, Russian. Open a fresh gallon of chablis."

Signor Orsini warned Adam that his responsibilities included giving all workers a glass of wine or a small soda for lunch. Americans called everything soda: Coca-Cola, 7-Up, Pepsi, and other sodas. But here was a gallon of chablis.

"Guys, the boss said having one glass is only possible."

"You Russian? You do not drink as we do? Italians need two or three glasses for lunch and some conversation."

"And if the boss finds out?" Adam did not want to quarrel with the guys and looked questioningly at Issidoro.

"Two or three," he clearly stated, "it's okay."

At lunch, spaghetti with tomato sauce and parmesan cheese was served. All Italians ate pasta with a piece of bread, dipping it in the sauce. Adam ate his serving without bread.

Chef Carlo asked, "Russian, do you like Italian cuisine?"

"Yes, I do."

"Look, Russian, do you know chicken Kiev? Can you make it?"

"Chicken Kiev? Of course, I can."

Carlo's eyes lit up. "This is great. I've wanted to learn it for a long time. Let's go to the kitchen. You can show me how to do it?"

"Carlo, let's, not today," chimed in Issidoro. "It's the first day he is working here. He still needs to check the bar downstairs."

After lunch, they went downstairs. To Adam's surprise, Issidoro turned on the light and opened another dining room reserved for luxury dining, absolutely different from the upper one for business lunches.

The elegant dining room was decorated in Empire style: antique sofas, columns, and monograms on the walls—a massive painting with an Italian landscape; people in national costumes collected grapes. There was a wide countertop of a huge bar. Narrow wooden lattice partitions between the bar and the tables created a feeling of intimacy and comfort. All was very theatrical, grandiose, and *molto Italiano*.

"Adam, check everything at the bar. Say if you will need something. I'll go upstairs and nap for half an hour," Issidoro yawned.

Adam went behind the bar and carefully studied everything. It seemed more luxurious than the top floor. A bar cabinet with a mirrored back wall was full of bottles reflected in the mirror, creating the impression of even more significant amounts of alcohol than there were. All the bottles had special plugs to measure serving shots. Adam translated this word as "shot." A shot was one ounce or twenty-eight milliliters.

The alcohol included whiskeys, aperitifs, cordials (the after-meal drinks), cognacs, and liqueurs. Adam decided to try one of the beverages each day. After all, he had to know his trade. *Am I a bartender or not?*

A small cooler behind the bar kept white wines, champagne, and various grades of beer. Red, dry wines lay in a special box above the counter at right angles. There was a deep sink for washing glasses, a metal shelf, and an ice maker.

Adam remembered his lessons from Gino and his words that the markup on alcohol in establishments ranged from 500 to 1,000 percent. Compared to this cheap stuff, the price of the expensive stuff seemed so unfair.

At the back of the bar was a square hole covered with a small wooden door. Adam poked his head in and saw a utility room and a table with a cash register. Yep, there would be a cashier.

He checked the machine for making ice, the fridge, different glasses, wine glasses, and other accessories. Everything was spot-on. He thought then he might go to sleep before taking the evening shift. He went upstairs and realized that the Italians could not say goodbye to the perception of a siesta, even after years of living in America. The entire crew was in sweet sleep, lying on chairs. And Adam, without thinking twice, followed their example.

Dinner at Orsini's

AMERICANS DID NOT USUALLY EAT "SUPPER." In the US, supper is considered a light snack before bedtime if eaten late at night.

What Russians called "dinner" was lunch in the United States. Dinnertime in the United States was between six and ten in the evening. At Orsini's, the lunch menu included appetizers and a main course. Drinks and desserts were required components. Dinner was more of a celebration than just a regular meal. Traditionally, only those who reserved tables came into restaurants.

"Issidoro, what happens if people enter from the street? And without a reservation?"

"No, we have no room," he proudly answered.

By six in the evening, everything was ready to receive guests. Maître d', Nino stood at the entrance, anticipating customers. The coat check room was next to the entrance, where a young lady with lovely earrings read a book during her last few free minutes. Orsini leased the checkroom, so it was entirely her business. She also sold some cigarettes, and selling them was profitable too.

Just outside the coat check room, Issidoro stood at attention with the dining room waiter, his right hand. A kitchen waiter and a busboy waited at the bar. Mario, with his team, was shadowed at the dining tables. Adam unwittingly noticed as all the details were worked out.

The first guests opened the door, and Nino smiled dazzlingly.

"*Buona sera*, Signore and Signora Smith!"

"Long time no see. I think it's been half a year?" Issidoro stepped up.

"Dear, you see, they recognize us! Do you remember us, Issidoro?"

"I will never forget my customers, Mrs. Smith."

"Oh, Issidoro! Last time, I was in awe of your pasta. It was called—" Mrs. Smith snapped her fingers and looked questioningly at her husband. "Honey, don't you remember?"

"Madam, you tried the spaghetti primavera with broccoli, fresh *pisseli* [green peas], carrot, and cream sauce. Would you like to order the same dish today?" wondered Issidoro.

"Oh, my dear, he remembers what I ate!"

"I told you, darling. Issidoro is the best."

Issidoro invited the pair to the table and led them to sit on the antique sofa.

"Come in, come in, Mr. and Mrs. Smith. We have a special for you today. *Vitello Piccata. Molto bene!*"

All this was happening in front of Adam. Standing behind the bar, he did not doubt that all the action was an entertaining show of excellent quality, and Issidoro was a great actor. Still, Adam had one question that bothered him. He called Yugoslavo and quietly asked, "Listen, does he remember who is who and what they ate?"

"Issidoro has a phenomenal memory. He recognizes people who have not come to us for a few years and remembers what they ordered."

"But it's impossible!"

"He remembers, and people specially come to be astonished by it. Issidoro earns more money than anybody else, thanks to his memory."

A busboy served breadsticks and olive oil on a small plate at customers' tables. Offering a menu right away at Orsini's wasn't acceptable because this supposedly hinted to the customer to rush through faster service and say goodbye.

How can I understand this logic? In Russia, we should give people a menu immediately, or they will start to complain. Here customers can enjoy a drink and dip the breadsticks in olive oil. Russian people first want a drink and food to eat and then talk. Here they have time to talk.

Adam was amazed by this difference in habits adopted in America.

"So, you're good? How's our olive oil?"

"Just simply wonderful, Issidoro."

"Want to look at the menu?"

"I'm afraid, Issidoro, you already know what we will eat today."

All three laughed.

"Mrs. Smith will enjoy the spaghetti primavera and, for you, gorgeous veal piccata.

And for the appetizer, I will make an excellent Caesar salad you will share. *Bellissimo!*"

"Yugoslavo," whispered Adam, "what's veal piccata?"

"The same as *vitello piccata* at lunch, our signature veal dish."

After Issidoro made his traditional speech, he offered Orsini's wine list wine.

"I recommend this special wine, the Santa Margherita Pinot Grigio. We have it exclusively. Very light, crisp, and pleasant."

Mr. Smith immediately agreed to that. A waiter came with a bottle of wine in his hands. He had a spectacular hand movement to show Mr. Smith the unopened bottle. He nodded, and with a spin, the bottle was opened. First, the waiter poured a symbolic portion for Mr. Smith. He rolled the glass and sniffed, and he sipped only after that. The waiter froze in anticipation of the process. Finally, Mr. Smith nodded approvingly, and the waiter filled their glasses to the halfway mark with the excellent white wine. The bottle went into a bucket with ice on a metal pole near the table. No matter how often Adam watched this ritual, he was always amused. Each one played the role with dignity in this little scene, and all were satisfied.

Soon Issidoro moved a service cart close to the Smiths' table; customers could watch every move. Adam, too, looked in that direction with interest.

The kitchen waiter started. He did not work directly with customers and delivered the necessary products to the show. In front of Issidoro, he placed romaine lettuce, three small anchovies in a glass bowl, toasted white bread cubes, spiced croutons with garlic, and a raw egg. Issidoro waved his hands like a conductor, and the presentation began.

The salad leaves went down into the big salad bowl. Anchovies were a necessary ingredient for the dressing, obedient to the hands of the maestro. With a fork, he transformed it into a puree. The raw egg was broken, and the yolk was extracted and mixed with the anchovy paste, freshly ground pepper, salt, and olive oil. Issidoro added the juice of a lemon to the resulting sauce and poured everything onto the lettuce. It was topped with croutons and generous tablespoons of grated parmesan. Then this splendor was masterfully picked up with a spoon and fork and placed on two plates.

The plates were presented to the customers. The audience approved it with applause, and Adam understood why.

The kitchen waiter delivered pans and pots with shiny lids, and Issidoro waved his hands over the mobile cart with two gas stoves. The busboy cleared the table and served clean silverware after the salad. The second act began. In the first pan, he melted butter. Then in placed spaghetti, boiled al dente, and all the prepared vegetables: sautéed broccoli, fresh green peas, and thin slices of carrots. Over it was generously poured half-and-half—a top-rated product in America- consisting of half cream and half whole milk. Issidoro gently heated the sauce with the spaghetti and sprinkled dashes of salt, freshly ground black pepper, and parmesan. *Voilà!* The pasta primavera was ready. At the same time, on the second stove, the veal piccata was prepared. A sauce of white wine was made; lemon was squeezed, and the sauce thickened and gently enveloped the veal. The obedient master, Issidoro, heated a broccoli side dish with garlic, carrots, and fresh green peas. It was graciously placed on the flat, warm plates, and the waiter put it in front of Mr. Smith.

And then there was the last stroke. The waiter held a long wooden peppermill.

"Would you like fresh pepper?"

The mill sprinkled tiny black spots over each plate.

The traditional *"Bon appétit"* was said, and the Smiths had a couple of culinary masterpieces. They admired the skills and talent of the maestro, and Issidoro was already trundling the serving table to the next guests. There was a new show to carry out, where he played the first violin with his orchestra.

At the second table sat regular customers—a young couple. Issidoro treated them with great respect, even more than the Smiths. They called for champagne Dom Perignon and Yugoslavo quietly poked Adam with his elbow.

"Well, Russian, now look carefully. The most exciting part of the show—will be the duet of *Issidoro and Dom Perignon*."

Issidoro solemnly, almost reverently, presented the label of the bottle of champagne to the guests and filled their glasses. The bottle went into the same bucket with ice, where the Smiths' half-empty white wine was already chilling.

The dining room waiters' duty was to ensure the glasses were never empty. But with Dom Perignon, Issidoro acted differently. Yugoslavo explained it to Adam.

"Now it will be the sacred vessel, and nobody except Issidoro can touch it. This fun happens every time. And then, when the bottle is about to be finished, watch for it with both eyes. Otherwise, you will miss out on the most interesting part."

The glasses behind the second table were barely empty.

Issidoro removed the bottle from the bucket and poured the sparkling wine that cost $500 per bottle. None of the waiters' teams even approached the valuable bottle. Adam looked at the check. There were two entrees, risotto con tartufo (truffles), at thirty dollars per serving. Adam had never tried risotto or truffles and couldn't say anything. He was hoping today to fill this gap in Orsini's. Issidoro usually made hot meals; one or two tablespoons remained in the pans and were taken to the utility room, where anyone could taste it.

The kitchen waiter appeared with the order for the second table. In the pan was precooked white rice, and in a small glass bowl, two tiny and ordinary-looking mushrooms floated in a strange liquid.

These are the famous truffles? What an ugly appearance.

Adam was surprised.

Issidoro put big pieces of butter in the rice and carefully added half-and-half, mixing little by little. Then he poured in the liquid from the truffles and added grated parmesan. Adam thought Italians added parmesan to pasta, salads, and even soup.

No question about it; it's a delicious cheese, but not everywhere.

When the risotto was laid out on the plates, Issidoro delicately sliced the truffles above the rice using a special little hand slicer. The waiter used this opportunity to offer fresh pepper, and then Issidoro followed with the whole team (including Adam) to the back room. But hopes were in vain: the leftover risotto had already gotten into the hands of Issidoro's wife, who worked behind the cash register.

Adam got back behind the bar just in time. Issidoro took the bottle of Dom Perignon from the bucket. He lovingly wrapped it in a white cloth napkin, and the guests' glasses were filled with champagne. And then—Adam couldn't believe his eyes— he deftly turned away from the customers, filled a giant wine glass full of champagne, and set the empty bottle back in the bucket with ice. He went out with the glass to the back room without turning around. Adam went there too. He had to see Issidoro drink.

He drank the champagne with such delight and enthusiasm that Adam could not resist saying, "Oh, and how is it, Issidoro?"

"The highest class!" He smacked his lips. "Although, honestly, I do like Taittinger Blanc de Blanc better. It's a little cheaper, but I like it more."

Adam could not keep this conversation up since he hadn't tried either one. They had hardly returned to the dining room when the man from the second table said, "Issidoro, pour us more champagne."

"Pardon me, guys, you drank it all." He extracted the empty bottle from the ice.

"Oh, yes? Then open another one for us."

Issidoro's cheeks got pink. He was already planning a second glass of his favorite champagne tonight.

Two bottles of Dom Perignon cost $1,000. Two plates of risotto, another sixty bucks. And then, 20 percent (and maybe more) was added to the order for the tip.

Adam did not understand these people from the second table. The rich do not understand the poor, and vice versa.

Mr. and Mrs. Smith enjoyed the chocolate mousse cake. Issidoro told Adam to pour two drinks: cognac and Bailey's Irish Cream.

"Don't put it on the check. It's on the house."

The evening was in full swing. All tables were occupied, and some visitors had to wait a while. They spent time at the bar, waiting for a reserved table. Adam spun like a squirrel in a wheel, barely managing to keep the guests seated at the bar and execute orders from the waiters. Nino watched the waiters and captains; all worked without stopping. It was a complete sellout when the boss, Signor Armando Orsini, came in. He immediately entered the dining room, greeted the customers, smiled at them, and joked with the regulars. He paid particular attention to the guests behind the bar and entertained them by talking until their tables became available.

On his first working evening, Adam was in suspense and confused. Signor Orsini had asked Issidoro to send some dinner upstairs. Adam learned that a luxury apartment was at the restaurant's top, where the restaurant owners stayed during shifts. The influx of guests only got lighter at half past ten, and the dining room seemed emptier.

The business belonged to two brothers, Armando and Guido Orsini. They worked in shifts: one week Armando, and next week, Guido. Based on conversations, they had different characters, good and evil.

Adam did like Signor Armando right away, and he needed to wait for fate to prepare him for his acquaintance with the second boss, who started on duty the following week. Yugoslavo claimed that they could not expect anything good from Signor Guido. But Issidoro did shake shoulders, saying, "Soon, you'll see him for yourself."

Chicken Kiev

THE PHONE RANG as soon as Adam entered the apartment late Saturday evening. It was Nata. She had taken her suitcase and was sitting in some railway station in Syosset on Long Island. Drowning with tears, she sobbed into the phone. The only thing Adam caught was that she had quarreled with her parents' friends and left them.

"And what is to be done now?" Adam realized that the question sounded stupid. "Well, stay there. I'll come for you."

The railway station was not far from his house. Igor had told him that trains went from there to Long Island. He had to find this girl before something happened, so he needed to buy a ticket to Syosset and get there in time to help this girl. It turned out to be more complicated. He went at night along a subway rail line running overhead. It was dark and scary, but that was only half the problem. When he finally reached Woodside train station and asked for a ticket to Syosset, the cashier broke out in a tirade where Adam understood only one word: *Syosset.*

He repeated, *"Syosset,"* and stuck a ten-dollar bill in the window.

The cashier talked, but he didn't understand her as she continued trying to get through to him. Adam smiled apologetically and stubbornly requested a ticket to Syosset. Finally, she gestured through her frustration and issued the ticket and change.

Soon the train came, and Adam sat down, happy everything was going successfully. He felt heroic, as he was on the verge of rescuing the poor, lonely girl from the clutches of danger in the New York night. Soon the train stopped, and all the passengers spilled out of the wagon. A railroad employee stopped in front of the bewildered Adam.

"This is Syosset?" he asked hopefully.

"No, it's Jamaica. The train will not go farther."

"How come this is Jamaica? And when is the next train to Syosset?"

"At four in the morning."

"Oh, God! And what do I do?"

"It's your problem, man."

Oh, yes! The cashier tried to explain it to me. And now I am stuck at night in Jamaica.

The first train would come in five hours. It was cold on the platform, and Adam decided to go to the small, deserted, dimly lit station building. All Adam knew about this area was that it was considered one of the most criminal parts of the city. He carefully skipped around a dangling, dark, gloomy figure of a man moving toward him.

At the train station, he saw a payphone and dug into his pockets; thank goodness, there was some change. The only one whom he could call in such a situation was Igor. He hated to do this, but there was no choice. Adam told him about the incident.

"Yes, you did not listen to me," replied Igor. "But I warned you not to be concerned with this girl."

"Listen, Igor; you asked me to help her in Vienna. And now, when she is God knows where, lonely, in a huge, dangerous city, I should have replied, 'Sorry, don't call me anymore'? I had to help."

"Oh, and how have you helped? I cannot help you. Come home on the first train and forget all about it." Igor hung up.

Adam got very angry with him, even though he was partly right.

Run into the night without knowing where—this is pure foolishness. It's a vast distance. Everyone only suffered. I should have told Nata that she needed to return home to those people, and tomorrow I could have phoned and come up with something. And now what? Hopefully, she is not getting mugged. I need to return home, act appropriately, and not be stupid.

Early in the morning, the train to the city finally appeared. Adam sat in the car and tried not to fall asleep and miss his station. Finally, Woodside was announced, and he jumped out of the car. He went back home under the noisy elevated subway overhead.

He was exhausted from lack of sleep, and sometimes it appeared he was about to fall asleep on the street. He finally got to his apartment. Never had his studio seemed to him so cozy and safe. He collapsed into bed and immediately fell asleep.

* * *

A loud ringing yanked him out of sleep. It was the phone. He took it for an alarm clock and jumped, terrified that he had overslept for work. But, no—today was Sunday, and the restaurant was closed. It was Nata on the phone.

"I've been waiting for you all night—"

"Nata! Thank God you're okay! I went for you, but the train stopped at Jamaica Station until the morning. I couldn't send a message to you. Where are you now?"

"At your house. I'm calling from downstairs."

"How did you find me?"

"Your letter had a return address on the envelope. I came here in a car."

"Who brought you here? What car?" Adam didn't understand what was going on.

"Can you come downstairs?"

"Oh, I'm sorry. Yes, of course, now."

Seeing Adam, Nata jumped out of the car, embraced his neck, and broke down in tears. The driver, a young man, pulled her suitcase from the trunk.

He shook his head and repeated, "It's horrible and dangerous to let a young girl be alone."

They thanked the driver for bringing her here. It turned out that she had paid the driver $150. And while Adam took the suitcase upstairs, she incessantly apologized, begging him not to throw her to the mercy of fate.

"I know it was dangerous, and I was not very reasonable. But I could not stay there. Besides, I do not know anyone here except you, Adam."

"Okay, okay. Well, all's well that ends. We'll think about what to do. Take a shower, and sleep for a bit. I'll go to the store and buy some food."

On the way to the shop, Adam pondered the situation.

Of course, I do like her. But there's a significant age difference; I'm forty—she's almost twenty years younger. Oh, it's so many problems could be now. I can forget the friendship with Igor, whatever it was now. I work, and I can feed the two of us. But what should I do with my plans for my business? I have a dream to open a small restaurant.

When he returned home, Nata slept serenely and woke up only in the evening. Adam had prepared spaghetti a la Issidoro.

"Are you hungry?"

"Oh, terribly! What's for dinner?"

"Italian pasta. I took the recipe from the guru of our restaurant. Nata, tell me what happened."

"I ... I don't want to talk about it now. Can I tell you later?"

Adam agreed and focused on cooking. He used a wooden spatula and fork to cook the spaghetti with butter, then added tomato sauce and half-and-half. In the end, Adam grated parmesan. However, as hard as he tried to do it the way Issidoro had, skillfully and beautifully, it didn't work out quite well.

Nata had barely tasted the pasta when she exclaimed, "Oh, my God! Adam, it's delicious."

"It's just because you are hungry."

"Not just that, it's also really very tasty."

"You want some wine? I have a white wine."

"No, I don't drink alcohol. Maybe Coca-Cola or something like that?"

Adam only had tea. Blowing on the hot drink, Nata timidly asked, "Will you send me away?"

He shook his head.

Capital of Immigrants

"Adam, I don't think you understand. I know I'm young. I want to be with you, and even in Italy, I thought about this a lot. And here I do like you very much. When you are near, I have nothing to fear."

Adam nodded and said, "I do like you too. I work and will be able to take care of us. And stop thinking about any fears. As you see, I have only one small room, but we can live here together."

Thus, began their first passionate night. It was a family. Adam worked, and Nata waited for him at night.

* * *

The next day, Adam waited to meet the second boss, Signor Guido Orsini. Waiters and busboys scurried back and forth, serving tables for lunch, crooking smiles at one another, and saying something jokingly about "a hard week." Nobody spoke directly about Guido Orsini, but Adam already knew that the second owner of Orsini's didn't seem to be respected here. For Adam, it remained a mystery.

Everything for lunch was ready, and Adam decided to clean the cooler for the white wine. He washed the big cooling flask. He gently disassembled it into parts and was amazed at how dirty the inside was.

"Yugoslavo, when was the last time my predecessor washed it?"

"I think he never washed it."

"How come?" Adam was sincerely surprised. "There will be insects in it soon."

He removed the dirt and washed and polished the big container.

"Look what this Russian did. He is good."

The crew admired his intention. It was time for lunch, and everything started to happen in the usual, crazy rhythm. Adam made drinks, cocktails, juice, and wine. He worked on the checks and called the credit card companies—in short, he did everything, as always. During lunch, Signor Guido Orsini appeared. He shook Issidoro's hand and checked out the dining room, vaguely nodding at rare acquaintances. It turned out to be the opposite of his brother. Armando, unlike Guido, was tall, slender, and elegant. He was always friendly and polite with employees and customers. Guido Orsini was short in stature and fat with a big belly. He always had a bad temper and expressed unhappiness. This brother looked like he had fallen and was sloppy.

The boss approached the bar. Adam understood that he had to behave politely and gently.

"Good morning, Signor Orsini."

Guido asked Issidoro, "Is this the new bartender? Can he handle the bar?"

"Yes, completely, Signor Orsini. He is fine."

Guido Orsini took another look at Adam and left.

Everyone breathed a sigh of relief, and Yugoslavo chuckled to Adam, "Well met."

After lunchtime in the kitchen, Adam met the chef, Carlo.

"Russian, you promised to show me how to cook chicken, Kiev? How about right now, while I have time?"

"I can," he agreed. "Only, please, Carlo, call me Adam."

They went to the kitchen.

"Meet Adam, *ragazzi*. That one is Agostino, our veal specialist. Niccolò is the youngest. And that is Alonzo; he's the sous chef."

Capital of Immigrants

"What is a sous chef, Carlo?"

"The next man in the kitchen after me. When I drop dead, Alonzo will take my place."

"You'll drop dead, Carlo? You will outlive us all." Alonzo switched to Italian. Carlo also started booming and gesturing, and Adam thought they were fighting. But soon, the noise lessened, and Carlo again turned to Adam.

"Russian ... uh ... Adam, don't be afraid. It's not a fight. We Italians like to make noise. The chicken fillet is already done." He nodded at the table where the cooled chicken breasts lay.

"No, these are not suitable. For chicken Kiev, taking a piece of meat along with the wing bone is necessary."

Adam took a whole chicken and showed how to carve the chicken breast properly.

"Cut the half of the wing and what's left on it; trim to the bone until it's clean."

"Well, it is a chicken breast." Alonzo was indignant.

"Alonzo, you have to listen to what people say, not—" Carlo added something in Italian. Everyone laughed, and Alonzo flushed and hurled an unkind look at Adam.

I've earned myself an enemy.

Adam continued aloud, "Now, we separate the small fillet from the large fillet. Then we cover both fillets with film and slightly pound them flat. Add salt, pepper, and fresh lemon juice. Next, we'll add a big chunk of butter and chopped dill."

"We have no dill, but we have parsley."

"Parsley is not good. Okay, let's start. We will make a small butter barrel and place it on the large chicken fillet. Then we'll put the small fillet on it and form everything around the butter so the bone sticks upward."

"You spend so much time just to make two chicken cutlets?" snorted Alonzo.

"That's why, Alonzo, you will remain a sous chef. You are too lazy to learn new things," said Carlo. "Come on, Adam. What's next?"

"Mix the eggs and milk to make *lezon*, as we called it in the Russian kitchen, and we need breadcrumbs."

"Alonzo, take two eggs and milk to make—how you said, Adam—*lezon*? Okay, now I will teach you how to make fresh breadcrumbs."

Carlo brought over a frozen loaf of white bread.

"Are these the fresh breadcrumbs?"

"I'll teach you."

Carlo turned on the machine with a grater and put the loaf through it to make crumbs.

"You see? It's fresh breadcrumbs, so it turns out tastier. What's next?"

"We roll the cutlets in flour, then the *lezon,* and then breadcrumbs. Then we fry it in deep fat till it's done. Before serving, we will put a paper cup on the bone. It will look prettier, and you can hold it in your hand."

Adam had to go. It was time to prepare the downstairs bar for the evening shift. And when he popped into the kitchen again, the chef had finished the chicken Kiev.

"How was it, Chef?"

Carlo made a ring with his index finger and thumb and kissed it. "*Bellissimo*, Russian!"

Penne ala Vodka

NINO WAS NOT ONLY MAÎTRE D' but was also an old-timer of Orsini's. He told Adam that their restaurant had been one of the first and changed New Yorkers' attitude toward Italian cuisine thirty years ago. And even then, it was one of the high-class restaurants. There were hundreds, if not thousands, of small Italian eateries, but none were at Orsini's level. Celebrities, movie stars, politicians, and prominent lawyers often visited the restaurant.

One evening, a very famous baseball player of Italian descent came in. Guido Orsini, with a flattering smile, welcomed the guest of honor. Adam knew nothing about baseball or baseball stars. Meanwhile, the entire staff went out to meet this idol.

"What will you drink, Denis? As far as I remember, you do like bourbon on the rocks? Bartender, a drink on the house for our guest." Adam tipped the bottle of pure corn whiskey over a glass with ice cubes.

The guest was sitting at the bar, waiting for his friend. The waiters ran to him, requesting autographs on baseball cards or pieces of paper. The star absently smiled until his guest arrived, and Issidoro invited them to the table. The baseball star left five dollars at the bar. Adam was pleasantly surprised and took it, believing it was an honestly earned tip. But Guido Orsini immediately emerged in front of him.

"You took the money Denis left? You must write it on the check and give it to the cashier. Did you not know that we collected all tips? That is how you get paid your salary, Russian."

Adam was frantic and barely suppressed his anger.

He's a skunk, this Guido. It goes to Armando, too; he is no better. I was so naïve. I didn't realize this when they gave me a paycheck. I earned the tips, and they collected them, which is part of my salary.

Guido continued, "Russian, you're not a union member? You must join. We have no right to hire nonunion members. Go to Nino; he will explain everything."

Adam frowned, but it was not the time for emotions and resentment.

Yugoslavo made an order: "A dry vodka martini straight up. Try to make everything right."

Adam mixed the drink in the shaker, and Yugoslavo took the finished cocktail but immediately returned with the glass.

"Customer said there is too much vermouth. And he wants the drink very dry."

Adam poured the cocktail into the sink and mixed a new portion with no vermouth, just pure vodka, and ice.

"Okay, take it now. It's dry beyond imagination."

But Yugoslavo again returned.

"There is still too much vermouth. He wanted it drier."

"The truth? Too much vermouth? Well, well. Wait here."

Adam pretended to prepare a new cocktail.

"That's it. Take it."
"But, Adam, this is the same one—"
"Take it, Yugoslavo, take it."
When he returned, there was no glass on his tray.
"Imagine—he said it is now correct; that's a dry martini. And I told him that the bartender poured no vermouth at all."
"Yugoslavo, are you stupid? You humiliated him. And what if this fool complains to our fool? Imagine how fast we would be fired."
"Yes, but I just couldn't hold off."
"Hold on to your emotions? Let's work. Spit, and don't pay attention. No time for sentiments."
Time flew rapidly. At 10:00 p.m., Guido reappeared in the restaurant with a woman. Issidoro covered a table for them, and all worked even faster under the direct supervision of the boss. The dining room was empty by eleven o'clock, but this couple continued to have fun. Signor Orsini and his companion were not hurried; they laughed and chatted. The whole team remained on duty. A second cook was on duty in the kitchen. Nino started a conference with Issidoro. Adam waited at the bar. Waiters and busboys gathered in the back room and grumbled that they had not been released to go home and had to start work again at ten in the morning. Issidoro came into the back room, and people immediately spoke angrily.
"Quietly, guys. I'm going to ask him."
He promised to return to tell them what to do. Adam watched as Issidoro, apologizing, smiled politely at Signor Orsini.
"Issidoro, what time is it? Is there anyone else in the restaurant?"

"Signor Guido, now it is 11:30 p.m. And nobody else in the restaurant now."

"Wow, how time flies. Well, then, we will go too."

He slowly got up from the table and ceremonially left, holding his lady under his arm.

Adam came home very late and caught Nata in tears.

"What happened? What's the matter? Did you talk with your parents again?"

"I … was afraid … you were missing. You were gone for a long time."

"That's the job, you know. Sometimes I have to stay longer."

"I understand, but anyway … I was afraid. I was scared."

"What are you afraid of, baby? I neither disappeared nor was lost. Tomorrow, I'll have to get up again and go to work. So, let's go to sleep already."

"Adam, I called my parents."

"So, here's the problem."

"Yes, and I told them about what happened, their friends from Long Island, and about you. They both cried and couldn't believe that people had let me down. When they came to Moscow, my mom and dad did many good things for them. And they promised that I would be like their own daughter to them." Nata again burst into tears.

"Well, well, that's enough. Tears do not help sorrow. It's not such a tragedy. I'm with you. Besides, don't forget that they are Americans, typical Americans. They love to smile and say wonderful things, but it means nothing. Your life—it's your problem."

"Yes, but in Russia—"

Capital of Immigrants

"We're not in Russia," observed Adam. "What did your parents say about me?"

"My dad said—after some years, I'll be still young, and you'll have nothing you can do—"

"It's about sex?"

"I don't know. We never talked about such topics."

"Nata, they are right. We need to think seriously about everything."

"Perhaps." She hastily added, "I just remembered. Someone named Alex called you. He left his phone number and asked you to call him back."

"It can wait until tomorrow. Come on, let's go to sleep. Otherwise, I'll fall asleep at work."

The next day, Adam asked Nino about the union for restaurant workers, and after lunch, he went to receive his official status. The union officer enlightened Adam about his rights and advertised their organization.

"We have a powerful union, and you will receive a paycheck from us if a strike happens. The salaries for people in the service sector consist of the tip and the minimum wage sum. By law, restaurant owners can pay less per hour than the minimum wage wherever people should receive tips. But they must pay no less than $1.50 per hour. The boss must declare how much tips the workers get per month. Then at the beginning of the year, every citizen of the United States fills out a declaration of income. The IRS—this tax service—checks for payment of taxes, and if you've overpaid your taxes, they refund you the money."

Adam tried to memorize all he heard and finally asked a question that had tormented him. "Tell me, did the boss have the right to take my tip?"

"No, but he must consider all the tips and declare them to the tax service. He must add it to the salary issued every week."

"Thanks. Now I see."

Adam paid the two-month membership fee and got the union member book.

* * *

On the way back to work, he called Alex from a payphone. They had met for the last time in Vienna.

"Adam, hi! How are you doing? Eugene and I are in Flint; it's near Detroit. Remember, we were going to be there? The town is nice, but finding a new job here is impossible if you lose the old one. We're thinking of moving to New York. What do you think?"

"New York is big; there are plenty of opportunities to work. Come over. I will help you to find an apartment."

"This is great. Who is that young lady who answered the phone?"

"My girlfriend."

"Are you getting married?"

"Well, I think we will."

"Congratulations, buddy. I think we will soon come to New York. Greetings to you from everybody."

When Adam returned to the restaurant, Nino was on guard at the entrance and asked, "Well, how did it go?"

"Everything was okay. I got an explanation for everything, but I did not understand everything. I'm a member of the union now and paid my dues. I've been told we got paid $1.50 per hour, plus tips. But I got paid only two hundred fifty a week; it didn't matter how much I collected in tips. The bosses declare all our income, not cash, all credit card payments. And if a tip is given in cash, then what?"

"Nobody saw who gave it and how much," replied Nino. "If no one saw, then you have not seen it."

"It's clear. Thank you, Nino. When I applied for the job, Armando told me they would pay me $250 a week. I thought tips would be extra, but now it's part of my paycheck."

"Be smart. Go to the bar now. Signor Guido already asked for you."

As soon as Adam took his position, the master appeared. He had a bottle of vodka with red flakes of chili pepper in his hands that generously filled a quarter of a bottle. Signor Orsini put it on the bar and nodded at Adam.

"We'll have a new dish on the menu, *penne ala vodka*. You are Russian, and you all drink vodka. Try it. Is it hot or not?"

"Oh, Signor Orsini, you want me to drink *that*?"

"Of course. It's not to sniff. I allow you to drink it."

Adam poured some vodka into a glass. Issidoro, watching the scene, laughed. "Hey, Russian, go easy on it!"

"And how will I know if it's hot or not?"

Guido Orsini liked this answer, and he howled. Adam had already noticed that he liked primitive humor and flat jokes. Adam drank the vodka, and his stomach was immediately on fire.

He noisily gasped.

"Very sharp. Russian stores sell pepper vodka, but the alcohol is 30 percent, not stronger. And this one, a real beast."

"What else is sold at Russian retail stores as an appetizer for vodka?" Signor Orsini was intrigued.

"Marinated mushrooms, caviar—red and black—and much more."

"Buy me that mushrooms and red caviar. I'll give you the money."

Issidoro tested the new recipe on the first customers.

"Today, we have pasta *speciale*, penne ala vodka. A pasta flambé."

"Flambé?" The guests and Adam, as usual, were surprised and intrigued.

The kitchen waiter brought two pans. One had short pasta with pointed ends—penne—and another had tomato sauce. Issidoro heated the penne with a piece of butter, splashed the pepper vodka, and tilted the skillet so the flames broke out inside it.

It became clear why this pasta was called flambé. The flame quieted, and Issidoro added tomato sauce, cream, and parmesan. All this was sprinkled with fresh black pepper and salt and nicely laid on two warm plates. It was a gastronomic spectacle. Maestro Issidoro, as always, ended with the loud applause of fascinated customers. The remnants of the new pasta dish were taken to the back room and solemnly tasted by the creator.

"So, tell us," his colleagues asked curiously.

"*Molto bene!*"

"Okay, make more next time. We all want to try."

Before working at this restaurant, Adam thought pasta was all macaroni products. It was called this way in the USSR—nothing special. Food for people experiencing poverty is not world cuisine or a delicacy. Having tried different pasta prepared with different sauces and fillings, Adam knew the preparation rules for spaghetti, penne, and fettuccine. He began to understand and appreciate good dishes. Pasta with seafood was a world-class dish. Of course, not every New Yorker could afford dinner at Orsini's. But Adam saw that Italian cuisine—even at the level of the eateries, fast food, and pizza joints—had conquered America and had become, arguably, the most popular cuisine.

Celebrities at Orsini's

SOME CELEBRITIES MARKED THE FOLLOWING WEEK at Orsini's. One evening, Sammy Davis Jr. came to have dinner with his agent. This brilliant musician, singer, and dancer was an amusing and straightforward guy. He joked right and left, answering questions and willingly interacting with the patrons. Adam, with unconcealed interest, looked at him. He was short. He did not show off his fame and gladly discussed his friendship with Frank Sinatra.

"My friends were Italians and got me accustomed to pasta. So, Issidoro, what will we have today?"

"Penne ala vodka, Mr. Davis. A new specialty."

"Oh, please, call me Sammy."

Adam shared his impressions about the star's visit with Nata at home, but she listened without interest. Lately, she had been brooding and quickly broke into tears. She was often sad and cried, especially after phone conversations with her parents. Adam was tired of calming her down but didn't know how to resolve this situation.

"In the end, what do they want? And what do you want?"

"They want me to go to California. Their best friends are in San Diego; they have a son my age."

"Perfect. Another best friend ... somehow with an adult son."

"Adam, we all have been friends and lived near each other. My parents want me to go; they fear the Russian government will not let them go. My mom worked on a secret space project and was awarded a medal."

"Well, now, everything is clear. No wonder your mom is not allowed to leave the country."

"Mom now has become very religious, and she cries every day. She blames herself that she threw me at those people from Long Island. They have two daughters my age and wrote that I would be like a third child to them. But when I arrived a few days later, they told me I had to move to the college dormitory. It turned out that there was no space available, and I had to rent a room in the neighborhood with another girl. They helped me draw up a student loan, where I had to live and pay rent and tuition. Before leaving, those people gave me $50 and said they hoarded the money for their children and that it was intended for their college."

"You can only blame them for what they promised your parents. Why didn't they say, 'Send your daughter, and we'll help?' I find all those speeches about a third daughter pure baloney. And what if the California friends are the same as those from New York?"

"No, they're different. The best friends of our family."

Adam looked at Nata and understood one thing: her parents would not rest. They only knew one thing about him: he was older than their daughter by twenty years. And that was far from ideal. Discouraging Nata would only cause tears and suffering that would flood the apartment. Perhaps the truth was that it was better to let her go to San Diego. And if it proved not all that beautiful, she might come back.

"Nata here's what I think about it." Adam selected his words. "I work from morning till night. You spend your days sitting at home and crying. Your daily conversations with your parents have you crying more. We'll try it and see if they think San Diego is the best alternative. If friends supervise you and your relatives can eventually leave Russia, all will end happily."

"Do you want me to go there?"

"No. But when everyone is constantly crying, life becomes a nightmare. You will be there for some time. The telephone here is working; we will continually communicate. And if there are problems, you can return at any moment."

It was a hard decision for them. Adam realized he could lose Nata, but it was impossible to live in perpetual stress. As an adult, he realized that her parents would likely never be released from Russia. But he could never say that to Nata. Her illusory hope of meeting with them gave her the strength to live and wait. They decided to book a flight for the following Sunday. With some sadness, Nata told her parents the good news, and Adam noticed that she became happier and happier.

The next day at Orsini's, the famous actor Kirk Douglas arrived for dinner. Adam had seen the movie *Spartacus*. Although Mr. Douglas was already old, he still retained a proud posture and passed through the restaurant as if playing one of his roles.

One of the guys whispered to Adam, "He's one of yours."

"What do you mean, of ours?"

"An immigrant from Russia. And he is a Jew."

Capital of Immigrants

"Spartacus is from Russia? It can't be! And he is a Jew?" Adam always said he was Jewish, but everyone stubbornly called him Russian.

"In the USA, nationality goes after citizenship. You are from Russia means you are Russian. Jews are a religious group. Are you religious?" Nino was serious.

"No, but in Russia, being Jewish was a nationality."

"Maybe in the Soviet Union. All who come from Russia are Russians. Here in America, the Jews are the ones who observe the Jewish religious laws. You seem to have not seen these Jews yet."

The real Jews Adam had seen in Williamsburg.

"Adam, for next Friday, dinner will be an open bar for an hour and a half." Issidoro was excited. "We have next week a big reception for some VIPs."

"What does it mean, 'open bar?'" Adam was embarrassed by his ignorance.

"This means that people can enjoy any drink from the bar, whatever they want and how many they want. Just remove the most expensive cognacs and champagnes. For the tables, we serve Amarone Bertani wine. That is a costly wine. Let's go; you'll help me carry boxes. We will have distinguished guests and even Signora Gina Lollobrigida."

"The same one from the movie *Fanfan la Tulipe*?"

"And *The Hunchback of Notre Dame* and many others. Yes, this is her."

"Wow! That's not a dream? I can see such beauty in my real life?"

"You'll see. Take a box, and let's go."

People gathered at the door that evening and then walked to the bar. They ordered drinks and shuttled from group to group, communicating with friends and having small appetizers from the buffet. Adam noticed Gina Lollobrigida immediately when she entered. Armando Orsini personally led her to the bar, and Adam had the opportunity to verify Issidoro's words.

Nino had told him Armando was a ladies' man and still the Casanova, although he was late in his years. Signora Lollobrigida, despite her age, looked great. The title of the most beautiful woman in the world was fully justified, and Adam watched her with admiration. Armando Orsini gallantly offered her a drink. Gina smiled at Adam and asked for a glass of red wine. While she talked to Armando and responded to numerous compliments from all sides, Adam secretly enjoyed her sitting so close.

Well, what a beauty!

He had no words. He regretted that he could not take a picture of her. It was unforgettable to see her so close, the idol of his youth, and get a smile from her.

At home, it was the day of Nata's departure. They said goodbye at the airport, and Adam repeated, "If something goes wrong, immediately call. I'll come for you."

* * *

She was swallowing silent tears and embraced him tightly. Walking away, she turned and waved. He waved back. Adam understood that there was no other way. She left, and he felt relief. He had done the right thing. Otherwise, her parents would call daily, demanding to send her to these questionable friends in California. Nata would be crying for days on end. And the guilty one would be Adam. And now—it was not clear what to do now. Maybe it was all wrong? Who could be the judge of it? However, it was done for now. He must think about his business.

* * *

Time passed, and there was nothing new at Orsini's. Adam remembered Gino advised him, "In America, you need to develop a credit history with the banks if you want to be in business. Only then can you get credit for your businesses. First, take a small amount and always pay it off on time. When the debt is paid in full, take out a new loan. It is essential to pay on time. Make one error, and your credit history is down the drain."

Adam had already developed some credit history. He took a modest loan at the bank twice and paid it in full. Indeed, a small personal loan would be granted when Adam decided to borrow again. The main questions remained: what business did he want to open, and how much money would he need?

Meetings in New York

NOTHING NEW WAS GOING ON AT ORSINI'S, and Adam was bored. He wanted to move forward, but a well-thought-out business plan still did not come up. He couldn't start anything without a bank loan, even in a small space. Adam saved a small amount of money, a total of $10,000.

With Nata, everything was too foggy. She found work as a draftsperson at a local company. The parents' friends moved her to a rental apartment because she was a "bad example" for their growing son, who dreamed of being free and independent. These "friends" continued complaining about Nata, and things were not working out. They often spoke on the phone, and Adam knew things were not going well.

Nata tried to make the best of her situation through long conversations and joking with Adam. One of her stories described how her parents' friends' son used his earnings from a job at Mcdonald's to buy a used car without a windshield. They could only ride in it with sunglasses to escape the oncoming wind. All of it would be funny if it were not so sad. Adam missed Nata and thought some solution must be implemented in San Diego. If his fears for her unhappiness were confirmed, he would do something to bring her back. Her ever-crying relatives, sooner or later, must accept reality and agree that it would be better for her to be with him.

What would be the difference for them? Worry about a daughter who is in distant California or distant New York?

Adam continued to work and pondered the trip to San Diego. Once, in the evening, Alex called to invite Adam to a housewarming party. As it turned out, he and Eugene had already moved from Detroit for good.

"We rented an apartment in Borough Park, Brooklyn. There is a Jewish religious quarter there. A friend who has lived there for a long time helped us with the apartment. Come over here; we will sit, drink, and chat. Come on. We will be waiting for you on Sunday."

The following day, on the way to work, Adam bumped into an old buddy he had not seen for many years. Somehow, miraculously, immigrants from the USSR intersected in New York.

Adam had already gotten used to pleasant, unexpected encounters with old friends in that city.

Victor Stork had been a famous sous chef in one of Leningrad's restaurants. They knew each other very well, and in those old days, Adam was the general manager of a famous restaurant. Victor worked as a cook on a steamboat, *Pushkin*, sailed abroad, then worked at the Russian Embassy in India. He later managed to work as a cook, even in Antarctica. In general, Victor was a great, talented chef. He made good money and was able to buy a car, a model called the Volga. At that time, having a car in Russia was a huge privilege.

After friendly greetings and exclamations, Victor introduced his companion.

"Boss, this is Will Freeman. Have you heard of him?"

"Come on, stop this 'boss' crap. Of course, I heard. Hi, Will. The youngest chef of a famous Nevsky restaurant. How are you doing?"

"I also heard about you, Adam." They shook hands.

"Boss, what are you doing now? Where do you work?"

"Victor, please stop this nonsense. I'm no longer a boss. In Russia, I was. But here in America, I'm just the bartender."

"The bartender position is great. We've been here long but have not found work yet."

"You want me to ask my boss? Maybe we need cooks. I'll call you if I learn something. Give me your number."

At the first opportunity, Adam asked that question of Armando Orsini. He was surprised.

"Why does the Italian restaurant need a Russian cook? But maybe I can talk to the owner of the Russian Tea Room. Do you want me to do it?"

"Of course. Thank you very much, Signor Orsini."

Adam had heard about this prestigious restaurant. By a twist of fate, it was located back to back with Orsini's and next door to Carnegie Hall. The Russian Tea Room had appeared in the thirties and had initially been an institution where Russian immigrants—actors, ballet dancers, musicians—gathered. The owner hired a young American provincial girl to work in the coat check room. He was so enchanted with her charm and energy that he could not resist her, and they married. He soon died, and under the strict guidance of the new proprietor, the Russian Tea Room had evolved into a luxury establishment, the most popular and one of the most expensive restaurants in the city. Creative geniuses still went there, but different musicians, artists, and performers visited the expensive restaurant with bigger purses.

Signor Armando handed Adam a note: a recommendation letter to the restaurant owner and a phone number the next day. During the lunch break, Adam called Victor.

"Hi, you've heard about the Russian Tea Room? There is a chance to get to this very famous restaurant. My boss spoke to the owner. You need only to call and come in for an interview. Write down this number, and meet me at work for a recommendation letter. I'm here until late."

In the evening, Nino called Adam to the lobby. Victor and Will were outside.

"Hi, guys. Here's a note to the owner. Victor, why are you so gloomy? Not happy with that restaurant? That is a great opportunity for you."

"I do not know. I should see how it's going to work. Will and I want to open our own business."

"And who wouldn't want to? But first, you need to save some money. The Russian Tea Room—it's a dream. My boss told me they needed Russian cooks and now employ many Latinos."

"How do I communicate with them? I know a couple of words in English. And there are the Latinos."

"You're the cook. Just show them how to cook Russian food. Okay, guys, I must go. Good luck."

Adam returned to the bar. He didn't understand how Victor could be sluggish and displeased. He had gotten a rare chance to work at a famous restaurant in New York, and he thumbed his nose.

Well, it is his business to deal with it. If he doesn't want to work at the Russian Tea Room, it's his problem. To succeed, he has to plow as a draft horse in America. To me, it's stupid to lose such an opportunity.

On Sunday, Adam went to visit Alex. Getting off the subway station, he strode the streets, checking the address on the paper and wondering how he would like this quarter of town. Considering what to bring as a gift for the housewarming, he bought a beautiful cookware set.

* * *

This part of New York was so different from others. Everything changed utterly.

The streets had a crowd of men, and all wore beards, black costumes, and black hats—the uniform for religious Jewish men. They chatted among themselves in a language that was incomprehensible to Adam. The women were in long, dark dresses. Their heads were all covered with scarves. Kids in their outfits seemed exactly like miniature replicas of adults. The small boys did not wear black hats, and their dense, curly hair was covered with a small headdress. Adam felt uncomfortable, as if he had entered an alien world without invitation, but nobody paid attention to his clothing or the absence of a hat.

Alex and Eugene welcomed Adam as vital guests. They drank a lot of vodkas, and conversations circled work and viable business ideas.

"We need to save money, guys. That's now the most important thing," mentioned Adam.

"Adam, where is your girlfriend who responded on the telephone?"

"She is now visiting friends in California."

"You have to introduce us when she returns."

"Of course. And with a nice meal, we'll have a party. You are all invited."

Adam somehow got drunk without even noticing, whether meeting with old acquaintances or because of the conversations about Nata. Everyone perceived her as Adam's girlfriend, and his heart shrank in anguish when he thought about her. Finally, it was time for Adam to go home. Alex volunteered to walk him to the subway because Adam was a little drunk. He staggered up to say goodbye.

"Are you okay, Adam? We drank pretty well."

"Don't worry, Alex. It's not the first time I've gotten drunk."

"Not the first and not the last! Come on. Call me when your girlfriend comes back from California, agreed?"

"No problem! We definitely will."

He fell asleep on the way and barely woke up at his station. And when he reached the house, the first thing he did was call Nata.

"Hi, remember me?"

"Adam, what's wrong with you? Everything in order?"

"Perfectly. I've been visiting Alex."

"This is the one friend you said drinks always?"

"Yes, we used to do it often. I told him about you. He is eager to meet you."

"I don't mind, but I'm in California."

"I'll come to visit you."

"Are you serious?"

"You don't want me to?"

"I do very, very much want you to."

"Then it's all agreed. I must ask my boss about a short vacation, and then I will call you and tell you when my flight is."

Adam hung up and immediately fell asleep without undressing. The ringing alarm clock woke him up with a dreadful headache. A hot shower brought his tangled thoughts into relative order.

Oh God, I was so drunk. I promised Nata I'd come. I can't take it back. I have to ask for a break from work.

It was more than a week before he went to San Diego. His sister, Sonya, and her son, John, came to New York. Adam had to meet them to help them find an apartment and settle them at the new location. But the day of departure came, and Adam, impatient to meet up with Nata, flew to California.

San Diego

THE FLIGHT TOOK FIVE HOURS. Adam got three days off but was essentially left with only two after traveling time. He was surprised to learn that San Diego was California's oldest and second-largest city; however, there was no time for exploring historical and geographical details and points of interest. He went there for the sole purpose of finding out if Nata was happy.

She met him at the airport, and from the beginning, all became clear. Nata did not hide the tears of loneliness, fear, and fatigue. She could not believe that Adam had come, and now she was aglow with a happy smile, like a baby.

They could not stop talking for twenty-four hours after his arrival to compensate for the lost time. And with each passionate moment, Adam was more convinced of his loyalty to his decision: Nata must return to New York.

"In general, everything is clear. To stay here is pointless. Work as a draftsperson can be easily found in New York. After their release from the USSR, your relatives can come to New York. The day after tomorrow, I'm returning and will look for a new apartment."

"The day after tomorrow? So soon?" Nata was disappointed.

"They did not want to give me even three days. We'll be together again soon. What should we do here?"

"We can go to Disney Parks. It's so beautiful."

Lord, the Disney park. She's a child and therefore wants to go to an amusement park. Adam felt hit in the heart. *She is fragile, naïve, vulnerable, and thrown into everyday problems and turmoil. She was a shy little girl who grew up in a loving family, painted pictures, and attended college. Her previous life was great and cheerful. There were big celebrations and holidays. And now she is grieving for relatives.*

He desperately wanted to return her to her world of serenity and happiness.

"If you want, let's go to Disneyland."

They walked and rode the carousel. Adam thought he was obliged to make her stop crying. She enjoyed the whole day.

* * *

He remembered the time spent with Nata in San Diego on the flight to New York.

They had discussed their plans and how they would be.

"Nata, you should quit your job and warn the landlord. That can help you get the deposit back with no future obligations. I wouldn't tell your relatives; you can tell them everything from New York."

"No, I can't. I don't want to upset my mom."

"It will be disturbing. But if you say it now to your relatives, they will prohibit you from leaving. You will start weeping all over again."

Capital of Immigrants

"No, no, Adam, you don't know my mother. I will tell her I'll be much better with you, and she will not object. You'll see."

"Okay," he reluctantly agreed. "Just call me immediately after the conversation with your mother."

On the flight, Adam mulled over what they had discussed and thought about his future. He first needed to rent an apartment with more space and appeal. His studio must be changed. Then he would help find Nata whatever she wanted to do. It was wrong to be at home alone. The constant calls to the parents always ended in tears; it could turn anyone unhappy. Next, it was time to change jobs. He needed to make more money and buy a car. It would shape their lives and generally make them happier. Nata was just twenty years old, and she wanted something more entertaining. He should take care of this. Yes, that was what he wanted.

Adam spoke to the guys about his plans and the new apartment, and everyone agreed that Forest Hills in Queens would meet his demands.

"It's clean, beautiful, and quiet. There's a subway nearby. Go browse," advised Nino. Adam decided to do so on the weekend.

Work had undergone some changes. Issidoro had bought a house in Naples, where he was born, and his wife, Orsini's cashier, had gone to Italy to prepare the new housing. Everyone was curious about how much money Issidoro had laid out for the house, and when he admitted that the house cost half a million dollars and all in cash, everyone gasped.

"Where did you get so much money?"

"I worked here for twenty-three years. I have been working days and nights at Orsini's and saving up all this time. Nino also bought a house in Queens, Astoria. How much did you pay for your house, Nino?"

"I paid the same amount as you, but there is no comparison. I have a mortgage, and I must pay and pay. And there was no money to save. Me and my wife, we're both working."

"Nino, whose wife got a diamond ring last month?"

"Well, this is another story. I didn't tell you? She deserved such a gift, and I was responsible for buying it. I had long known Astoria's jewelry store owner and asked him to pick up a good one-carat single-stone diamond ring. He assured me that he had a handsome stone at a low price. I bought it and then decided to check it up and have the ring assessed. I paid $100 for an appraisal, and it turned out that my buddy, the jeweler, overcharged me. I brought him the estimated certificate, and he returned a substantial amount. So, nobody should rob me."

Adam remembered this story of the jeweler. Not that he had the money for diamonds, but everything in life could be helpful. The story of the departure of Issidoro and his wife had consequences; on the same day, Armando Orsini called Adam to his office.

"Can you maintain work as a cashier and bartender?"

"I think I can. But it's hard work in this mode. Every day from morning till night."

"We will find another bartender for lunch, and you shall do only the evening shift. Plus, I will add fifty dollars a week, okay?"

Adam agreed, and he shared the news with Nino. He nodded approvingly.

"Not bad, but I would, in your place, have bargained for more money."

"Well, I could ask for twenty-five dollars more per week. But this money would be more of a hassle all day long. No, I do not want to. Let's look for a bartender for lunch."

"Listen, Adam, I can put my son in this place. I have to talk to Armando."

Everything fell into place. Niccolo, Nino's son, began to work upstairs during lunch. Adam could come to the restaurant at 5 p.m., looking for an apartment during the daytime. Soon Nata phoned with good news: her mother had allowed her to return to New York. Another piece of good news was that Nata would arrive in two weeks. It became clear that searching for a new apartment should be done quickly. Adam liked one house on Queens Boulevard. It was a residential complex of three high-rise buildings shaped like a big ring, and inside it was a fountain.

The apartment on the sixth floor was great—light and empty; it had a fountain view. It was twice the cost of the old rental studio. But Adam had received a salary increase, and he had already imagined the wondering eyes of Nata, which would light up when she saw this apartment. The question of housing was solved.

Forest Hills

AS NINO HAD SAID, the area of Forest Hills in the borough of Queens turned out to be beautiful and well-kept, with lush greenery. There were no old factory buildings or dilapidated brick monstrosities of architecture. In that part of the city, high-rise houses were mixed with private ones, and people lived decently.

The new housing was at an intersection on Queens Boulevard, where two other streets crossed. That reminded Adam of the famous place in Leningrad called Five Corners, a memorable place for him. In his past, Adam had overseen a network of eateries located around these Five Corners. The businesses included a restaurant, a huge bar, a bakery, and different fast-food establishments in the city center. But that was in the long-gone past. Now he is a bartender and looking for a nice place to live.

Queens Boulevard was incredibly long. Adam managed to explore the section from the Fifty-Ninth Street Bridge, thanks to the still-memorable strike of subway workers and his daily hikes to Roma di Notte Restaurant and back. The bridge linked Manhattan and Queens, one of the boroughs of the Big Apple.

Closer to the bridge in Queens was an area that was not clean and cozy. Many buildings stood abandoned with no signs of life

Capital of Immigrants

as they looked at a growing New York City with empty, dead-eyed windows. On the right side of the bridge was an area with buildings housing warehouses or factories, huge garages, and Pavilion Film Studios. On the left side of the highway were high-rises and entire neighborhood projects at the East River—free housing that the state provided for people experiencing poverty on the welfare program. Young single women with children and those from Latin America, Africa, and other troubled regions fell into the welfare trap and became those who were then called "the lost generation." Disadvantaged families received free housing, food stamps, health insurance, and many other privileges. If a single woman became pregnant, she had the right to a child allowance on the welfare program until the child became an adult. After that, if the child went somewhere to study, funding would be extended until the end. By then, the woman would be about fifty years old, and the state agreed that the person without a profession could not find a job after this age. So, they would get an allowance until the end of life.

A simple calculation showed that people should earn no less than $40,000 in income and be equal to those who benefit from the welfare program. There was no reason to struggle. Someone could get social benefits even without working at all. High crime, drugs, and drinking problems were integral parts of life around government welfare housing projects. Were those projects naturally established for dysfunctional families, for being on welfare-program people?

This neighborhood called Astoria was first after the bridge. Contrarily, a central part of Astoria's population drastically differed from its neighbors: mostly occupied by middle-class

Greeks and Italians. These diasporas did not mix; each group led its lifestyle and had shops, restaurants, clinics, temples, and churches. According to Adam, Astoria's projects were not as brutal as in other troubled areas, but that did not mean life and freedom. However, the welfare program influenced the area. There was free housing for those who settled there. His sister Sonya got an apartment in Astoria, but it perplexed him why she did not look for a job. Why did she not want more than she had?

The answer was simple: "I raise my son alone and don't want to work hard for peanuts. I'm quite happy with the welfare program. And I recommend you not disdain it. Some people are officially divorced but still live together for the benefit because it's so profitable. Yet, some still have a business. In our house lives Buba Kastorsky; remember that actor? Here he tried to work too. He gets some money, but most of the time, he does no work. And he still enjoys his life. But what about you? You wish to work. I don't understand it."

The welfare program, for Adam, seemed like a road to nowhere. The mere thought of this existence was hateful to him. Sonya didn't understand his aspirations. She couldn't fathom why someone would fight and work to prove something and build a business. After all, he could make almost no effort and get things for free.

What kind of life is it? Beg for help? Be poor for the rest of your life? That is not for me.

Queens Boulevard stretched further, and behind Astoria was a neighborhood called Woodside, which was adjacent to Jackson Heights. That was where Adam first rented a studio apartment.

Capital of Immigrants

In the 1970s, it was pretty safe; middle-class Americans lived there. But then the area began to change. Latinos arrived in the United States, legally and illegally, and occupied those territories, living in constant fear of getting deported. Authorities were aware of the situation; it could be why they arranged an amnesty every few years for those who had put down long roots on New York soil. Refugees who had lived in the country for many years were given official status. They could apply for jobs legally, and the state received taxes. As a result, it was a win-win situation for all.

The next piece of Queens was called Rego Park. Adam heard that many immigrants from Russia lived there. Most of them came from Leningrad and Bukhara, a city in the Uzbek Republic. This strange combination of different ethnic groups had created a large community, although incomparable to Little Odessa in the Brighton Beach area in the Brooklyn borough.

One primary avenue intersecting Rego Park was filled with Russian shops, a pharmacy, doctors' offices, and banks. Jews from Bukhara traded gold and carpets, and many people from Leningrad were the literary elite of immigration.

Adam walked around the area to get acquainted with its sights and possibilities for buying Russian goodies for Nata. All the rumors about Rego Park turned out to be accurate, and the first storefront he saw there had a familiar and straightforward title of "Monya's." The store was small and full of goods from the USSR: canned sprats, cod liver, cereals from Russia, and many sweets. It was nostalgic food for those who missed their abandoned homeland.

An older man behind the cash register was, apparently, Monya himself.

"Are you looking for something?"

"Oh, no. I was walking around, getting familiar with Rego Park."

"So, you are not a local. Then where have you stayed before?"

"I'm from Jackson Heights. Before that, I came from Leningrad."

"Here are a lot of people from Leningrad. Sergei Dovlatov often comes here."

"And who is he?"

"Seriously, you don't know? He's a writer, a highly revered one. And chief editor of the newspaper *New Americans*. A nice person. I like him, truthfully. But who doesn't like him?"

"Here in America, I have only seen one of our newspapers, *New Russian Word*."

"That is a very old one. Now everyone reads *New Americans*. Look on the counter. You can buy one."

"Yes, I will, but later. I'll be back on my way home."

Adam did walk down the street, looking at storefronts with showcases, considering different shops, and marveling at the abundance of Russian-speaking people. He noticed there was not a single Russian restaurant. Along the way, he came across a dimly lit vegetable shop. Adam saw a familiar face from Austria; he had eaten his first Viennese schnitzel in this person's company.

"Here you are. Nice seeing you, Janek."

"Adam! Long time no see. I'm so glad to see you."

"Same here. Are you working here?"

"Yes, this is my business. I put together all the money and some I borrowed. I work almost all day, sleeping for two or three hours. At night, I go to buy commodities to sell during the day. It's a bit hard, but I'm thrilled. Yes, and my family is here as well."

"Well done, Janek. When you pay off all debts, it will be easier. The beginning is the hardest part of the battle."

"I think so too. The start is always difficult. But I'm happy; it's a lot of work. Come over sometime. We'll chat."

"Of course. Good luck to you, Janek."

Adam moved on, jealous of Janek.

He's from the Uzbek Republic; those people are oriented to open businesses. Everything stays within their blood. They keep together and help each other.

Adam wandered under the next store signboard of "Glatt Kosher," a butcher's shop. The seller frowned and looked threateningly toward Adam, who felt unwelcome and quickly withdrew.

What is Glatt Kosher? I will need to learn that.

He crossed to the other side of the street and moved in the opposite direction. On the corner, directly opposite Monya's shop, hung a sign "Café." Inside was practically an empty room; it held a couple of uncovered tables. At one table, two men played chess. He saw an open door into the kitchen and heard voices. Adam thought he heard something familiar. Nobody stopped him.

He walked into the kitchen and saw the familiar faces of Victor and Will. Work was in full swing, and the kitchen was full of smoke.

"Wow! Hello, guys. Victor, what's up with the Russian Tea Room?"

"I quit. On the third day, I was gone from there. There were only Latinos. And I did not understand the crap they were saying. So, all the blame's on me."

Adam could not believe it and gasped. *Did he throw away that chance?*

"So, Will and I decided to do our own business," continued Victor. "We rent that kitchen to prepare and sell food to Russian stores in the Brighton Beach area."

"What do you cook?"

"Everything they ask for. Stuffed chicken neck, for example. Do you like that?"

"That old Jewish tradition. But this is not for me. And what other food can you do?"

"For example, *bigus*. You want to try?"

"Oh, come on, what is it, bigus?" Adam tried it. "Hmm, it tastes strange but delicious. It reminds me of homemade cabbage stew, but why are there smoked sausages?"

"Well, give it to the boss. With ham and smoked sausage. The traditional Polish dish, with smoked meat and sour cabbage."

"Huh? I did not know this. Who is the owner of the premises?"

Adam tried to turn the conversation to his advantage. "Some greasy guy. He wants to sell it to us. Asked five thousand bucks."

"Although, I think, for $2,500, he will surrender it," chimed in Will.

Adam decided to get into the game. "Guys, let's buy it and put a café here. We are all restaurant workers; we know this stuff. Five thousand dollars or, even better, 2,500—it's not the money.

Capital of Immigrants

I have ten thousand. If we spend another ten thousand, we can make a wonderful place. In this area, a lot of Russian people live. Well, what do you think?"

"Not good." Will shook his head. "For a full restaurant, it's not enough space. It will make a small café. What are the three of us going to do?"

"But in Rego Park, there are gobs of Russian people and no restaurant. People commute to Brighton Beach. Here is uncharted territory with marriages, anniversaries, birthdays, and banquets. Whether it's a little event or a meeting, these are often held at a restaurant, and I think we should open a café here and now. That is what everyone needs."

What Adam said made an impression on Victor. He liked the idea, but Will did not. Adam suspected that the last word in this business matter belonged to Will. Well, Adam would let them make the decision. In the beginning, Adam wanted to convince them that the idea of a small establishment could work, and he had already prepared a couple of arguments in favor of this, but he did not expect such an argument.

"Adam, everything is fine. But the main problem is that neither Victor nor I have money. With all his savings, Victor bought a pastry shop on Brighton Beach, which burned to the ground. We suspect he forgot to turn off the oven, which started the fire. Anyway, the result is the same; the money is gone." Will went silent.

"And there was no insurance?"

"Adam, you're kidding. What kind of insurance?"

"Will, you somehow stood well in the Nevsky restaurant. You should have some money saved."

He chuckled bitterly and said nothing, just walked outside.

"He came to America with his wife. And she took all the money he made," explained Victor quietly. "He has gone through hell. He did love this creature. Just don't mention those things. Even living with someone for a long time, you still know nothing about the person."

"How much money has he lost?"

"A decent amount. But, by the way, about the money. We do have a buddy; his name is Lev. This guy is in business and has a nice income. We have known him for a long time, even in Russia."

"Yes, Lev is a savvy guy," remarked returned Will. "He, along with his brother, made all kinds of deals. Lev already bought six taxi medallions, which means licenses from the city. In the beginning, he was behind the wheel at night. He bought a beauty salon for his girlfriend. She also earns pretty good money. Victor and I were at his house. Cool life. For one sofa, he paid four big ones."

"People with money—that's a good thing. But what will he do? You and Victor in the kitchen; I will be in the dining room, and what will he do?"

"He'll count money. He loves that," replied Will. "But if we want any restaurant business, we need more space. We should look at a place that has already adapted to our needs. We need a dining room for one hundred twenty to one hundred fifty people—some restaurants with kitchen areas, equipment, or something similar. Storage space, toilets, parking, and many other facilities must be available. And for all this, we need enough money. On the other hand, it makes no sense to start here; there is not enough return for everyone. So, your ten thousand, Adam, does not do anything."

Adam did not like Will's bossy talk; he behaved with some superiority and aspired to leadership. It looked like he would not be happy just in the chef role. Will dreamed of managing. Adam was not opposed to it.

If he wanted to be a leader, let him be. If things went well and business flourished, then who cares?

The outcome of this meeting was the decision to meet with Lev and see if the four people could agree.

Companions

ADAM CONTINUALLY DELIBERATED on how to open a business with the guys. He had known Victor for many years and had heard many positive things about Will as a professional in Russia. In his abilities, he was confident. In the Brighton Beach area, the Russian restaurant business flourished. The area was flooded with small cafés, taverns, small places, and giants such as Sadko, National, and Odessa. Why hadn't Rego Park organized something similar? Adam did not want to work in Brighton Beach. With its core group of immigrants, the local Odessa society differed from the other part of Russians. Its culture is at the root of the very different traditions of Russia's southern section. A mixture of Middle Eastern, Greek, and Mediterranean nations made peculiar characters. People were very energetic and strange. In Russia's literature and movies, Odessa town is usually considered criminal. After many months of communication with similar people in Zum Turken, Adam preferred to stay away from them. In the past, he was acquainted with Odessa's people, which contributed to Adam's unwillingness to work in such an atmosphere.

Many years ago, Adam and an old close friend, Andrew, visited Odessa on the Black Sea on their way to a famous tourist attraction, the Black Sea city of Sochi. They had to stop at the city of Odessa because Andrew wanted to sell extra seat covers for his new car. A new model had just appeared on the market, and someone told him that the local markets were suitable for selling such covers and that he could fetch good money for them.

Adam and Andrew were going to sell the covers and move further south. But everything happened so fast, even before they reached Odessa. They met a group of young filmmakers who were noisy and funny. They drank all the time. One morning Adam found himself in an unnamed "typical old" Ukrainian village that was chosen for filming. One of the restless filmmakers woke Adam at six in the morning.

"Adam, let's go freshen up."

Finally, after many days of unrestrained drunkenness, Adam got fed up. Moaning and grunting, he went out on the porch, thinking of washing his face with cold water. But his eyes were shocked at what he saw.

On the porch stood a big bottle of moonshine with clouded, homemade alcohol and three big glasses. His friend Andrew was intoxicated, contented, and had already had a couple of shots from the bottle. A large loaf of black bread completed the picture.

"You're bringing—" Adam panted. "My head is cracking, my arms are shaking, and you, monsters, are offering again—"

"Yes, don't be afraid. Have a shot now. It might make you feel better," said Andrew with a smile.

"Listen, we needed to get into this God-cursed Odessa long ago. How many days have we done the same thing? Every day we get drunk. Let's stop drinking for one day and finally go."

"Adam, everything is in order," commented the movie man. "Our crew also should be in Odessa tomorrow. Together we'll go. Come on, don't disgrace us in front of other people."

Andrew flashed his hand and poured the liquid into a glass. Adam drank the contents and immediately thought a pot of coals was in his stomach. It burned mercilessly, and Adam grabbed a piece of black bread and chewed to extinguish the fire.

"Sons of a ... you ... with your horrible homemade crap ... I drink no more. This homemade alcohol is disgusting. I can't even see it anymore."

Finally, they went to the vast and famous Odessa city flea market the next day. That famous market occupied a colossal territory Adam hadn't ever seen. Vendors were selling everything imaginable. There were huge, colorful Persian rugs, Bohemian crystals, fur coats, fashion clothing, and footwear. There were fake Lee jeans and dresses with labels that read "Couture from Paris." Everyone traded: venerable gentlemen, chic ladies, professional traders, and fashionable beauties. It was unlike the farmers' market in Leningrad, which was always quiet and peaceful, with old grandmas peddling sour cream and cottage cheese. There were guys from the Caucasus Mountains in wide caps. They raised a little commotion and created a natural Eastern bazaar: noise, uproar, pickpockets, and other traditional Eastern bazaar things. One word described it all—Odessa!

Andrew and Adam wandered around in the crowd with the seat covers on their shoulders until they finally sold them to someone at half price. However, they were satisfied with the sale, and Adam was happy to get out as soon as possible.

Capital of Immigrants

In general, the memories of Odessa did not encourage him to organize a business in Brighton Beach, where many people from Odessa now live. This area was well known as Little Odessa. It became famous for criminal activity of many kinds. Adam wanted to stay away from that area.

As planned, Victor, Will, Lev, and Adam had a meeting. Will spoke more than anyone else, and Adam realized he was not wrong in his assumptions that he wanted to manage the process.

"Victor and I will be principals in the kitchen," stated Will.

"Adam and Lev will engage in the dining room. A menu for banquets and other things must be arranged in advance."

"First, we need to solve the issue of capital," remarked Lev. "Adam will put in ten thousand. You, Will, and Victor have no money. I can give sixty ... well, a maximum of seventy big ones. That's eighty thousand. Divide by four. So, both of you will owe me twenty grand each, Adam ten. The question is, when will I get my money back?"

"First, we need to buy the equipment and accessories, and before we share any profits, we will pay you," responded Will.

"And if nothing is there to divide? What then, Will?"

"Lev!" Victor got excited. "Why do you start again? We already chatted about that."

"I want to know what happens if the business does not go. How do I get my money back?"

"We will all go to work and pay off our debts," offered Adam.

"We need to write an agreement to be legally correct."

All looked at one another and nodded approvingly.

* * *

That evening, Nata arrived from California. Adam met her at the airport and brought her to the new apartment. She admired its spaciousness, cleanliness, and coziness. The multicolored fountain in the courtyard seemed like a magic picture from a children's book.

"Oh, Adam, how wonderful this place is. So beautiful here. It probably costs a fortune."

"Not really," Adam lied cheerfully. "Come on. I bought delicacies, as you call them."

"Oh, how nice. I am starving."

Adam told her about their business plans and promised to introduce Nata to his companions. She fully trusted Adam's experience and believed in the importance of that project.

"But before I drown in this work, we may go somewhere to relax. It could be the Catskill Mountains; it's in the northern part of the state. Well, it would be nice to buy a car. But we will have to wait. Now all the money will go to the new restaurant."

Nata agreed. She was so tired of the fear that she wanted to listen to his voice and sleep peacefully. Adam looked at her and thought about how much she had to be worried during this time. He would now take care of her. And this responsibility was not only his burden, but it finally gave meaning to his acts. He now always had to consider that he had family and must keep her happy.

Sizzler Restaurant

A MONTH PASSED, and so far, the search for the premises for the new restaurant hadn't been promising. Such a small amount of money limited their options practically to zero. Adam perused newspapers and meticulously studied the headings under the business opportunity section, but there was nothing for the companions' money. Sometimes they gathered in Adam's apartment and pondered over responsibilities and business plans. Lev was almost always absent, recalling that he was not knowledgeable and had agreed to supply the money. Victor usually sat silently and drank tea.

Will spoke for a long time, using slogans and sounding very pathetic. "We must ... our business is obliged to ... the character of our company ...."

Nata nicknamed him "Komsomol Secretary," after the communist youth organization, for those lush speeches. Adam saw things were at a standstill; they wouldn't achieve anything with this approach. He amended his position. They should start with the small café and work their way up.

"Guys, let's return to the idea of a little café. We can occupy this small shop, and then we will slowly build it up. We'll open a large restaurant when we get on a solid footing."

Will was displeased.

"Adam, while we mess with the little café, someone will open a restaurant. And, admit it, there will be no need for a second place with Russian cuisine in this community."

"Will, we'll find nothing. Now we are simply wasting time."

Days went by, and the mood of the future business markedly changed for the worse. One day, Will's excited voice on the phone reported good news.

"Adam, there are some premises for rent on Queens Boulevard and 58 Street. It used to be a Sizzler restaurant, one of the branched-chain restaurants with two hundred seats. The real-estate agency requires $4,500 as a monthly fee, the rental price."

"Will, it is amazing! But what if we will not agree with the owner? Can we lose our money?"

"Well, but the real-estate agent will not show the property. First, we go to look, and if it is suitable, we will decide. He said the owner is willing to surrender the premises even today."

"Call Lev and arrange a meeting."

Soon the companions gathered nearby the real-estate office. They needed to decide on the property for rent. Adam started first.

"I've been once to this place when it was the Sizzler. It was a vast restaurant: the exterior looked fine, a large, one-story building. Parking is available. But what's necessary is to look inside. Let's go to the agency and get some details on it."

They went to the real-estate agency.

"Come, gentlemen. Get comfortable. My name is Allan. I represent the interests of the owner."

Will went first. "Allan, can you tell us why the previous owners closed the restaurant? What was the reason?"

"The reason is banal: bad management and financial issues. They owe a lot of money. They didn't pay rent for three months. Can I ask what kind of business you plan to open there?"

"We are all professional restaurateurs." Will again took the floor. "We want to do Russian cuisine because there is a large population of Russian people, and there are no Russian restaurants. Let us ask you, what are the terms and conditions for renting this place?"

"Rent the first year would be $4,500 per month. Each year will increase in line with inflation. The total duration of the contract is five years, with the option to extend by mutual agreement. Everything else is the standard rental agreement. You get the keys after the contract is signed and the first payment is received into the owner's account. My services are paid separately, and we will agree on confidentiality."

"Such as?"

"This means," continued Allan, "if the premises are not suitable for you, the landlord has the right to offer it to others, and you agree not to disclose the terms of our unsuccessful agreement."

Adam interrupted the conversation.

"And when do you get paid for the services?"

"Before we go to inspect the premises—that means right now. If you don't like it, you'll get your deposit back today."

"And if we'll need to think about it until tomorrow, then what?" wondered Adam.

"It must be today only. The owners don't like to waste time. We have plenty of applicants."

"Understood." Will came forward. "We want to discuss the issue."

"Please, of course. You can chat right here. I'll leave you guys here alone." Allan left.

"Oh, no. Guys, we better go outdoors to chat."

They went outside. Will and Adam were excited.

"Well, guys, what are we going to do? What do you think, Adam?" Lev was skeptical.

"I think we should go and see the place. If we don't like it, we get our money back today. Yet, we risk nothing. Are you ready, Lev?"

"You guys decide. I don't understand this business, and I'm responsible for the money delivered, that's all."

"Victor? Will? What are you going to say?"

Everyone agreed. The new business group returned and signed a confidentiality agreement, and Lev put $4,500 into Allan's safe. He said that the owner would be there in an hour. They went outside, quiet with their thoughts.

Witnessing the strange silence, Adam tried to cheer them up, but no one laughed. The money had been paid, and everyone understood it was a serious act. The time came when the decision should be made. It couldn't be washed away or laughed off.

Finally, Allan appeared with a nondescript type, more like a handyman than an owner of expensive premises on Queens Boulevard.

"Gentlemen, please meet Mr. Michael Blum, your future landlord, perhaps!" He laughed, pleased with his joke. "I told Mr. Blum about your plans, and he likes them. If everything is ready, you can get going straight away."

Allan cheered up, probably because of the prospect of excellent earnings. Indeed, it was a thumbs-up for anyone who can get $4,500 daily. That would cheer up even a grumpy person.

Capital of Immigrants

The premises were nearby. Mr. Blum pulled out a key chain, opened the front door, and shone a flashlight.

"Electricity is disconnected for nonpayment, but something will be visible with a flashlight. The toilets and storage rooms are below, and here is the kitchen area."

They went into the dark room.

In a shaky beam of yellow light, they saw pipes and wires remaining after dismantling the equipment. The visibility was close to zero; the weak flashlight didn't help. The only noticeable things were the walls and a large opening entrance to the kitchen area.

"Mr. Blum, where is all the restaurant equipment?"

"The former tenant left many debts. Everything was sold at auction for the repayment of debts. But the premises have the kitchen pipes, communication, and miscellaneous things left in place; connect your equipment. I have all the necessary documents and permits from the Department of Health, the fire department, and the Department of Buildings. Everything is constructed under the approved project and the sanitation norms."

"Thank you, we understand. We saw what we could. Now we need some time to think and come to a decision."

"Yes, of course, but do not take long; customers are already lined up in the queue. Call Mr. Allan when you've decided."

They said goodbye to Mr. Blum and went to the nearest café to discuss what to do next.

"Well, everyone understands that we have to decide now," began Adam. "Who wants to be the first? No one? Then let's start in a circle. Victor, you speak."

"Why me? I'm like everyone else. If you guys are for it, then I am too. And there is no other way."

Adam again wondered about Victor's passivity. It was as if he was not interested in the case's outcome. Victor always stayed away from the decision-making process.

Could we stay in business for a long time with such an approach? Maybe Victor is embarrassed by his business losses in the past.

"Lev, what do you think?"

"Guys, I am simply speaking as your lender. You decide. Adam, what do you think? Is it a good option?"

"I think this place has an excellent chance. We've found nothing better for that kind of money so far. It's large premises, excellent location for us. The location and flow of customers are what we will need. It's terrible, of course, that there was no light, so we could not see what repairs it may need. But it was a well-known restaurant. All engineering communications are there. Buying used equipment can save us a lot of money. And we can make the necessary repairs on our own."

"I also think it's a clever idea but with a little different approach," agreed Will. "We need to bring down the cost of rent to $4,250 per month. I think they're just bluffing about a queue of customers."

"And if they're not? What do we do then? This is pettiness," countered Adam. "I don't think he's bluffing. We must decide today; otherwise, we can lose our deposit."

"This is no pettiness; $250 a month is $3,000 yearly, Adam. This crafty Mr. Blum certainly will agree to reduce the price."

"And if not? What then? We risk spoiling relations with him and lose the premises."

"Adam, I guarantee you that he will agree. I will call him and bargain the price."

They argued for a long time, but changing Will's mind proved impossible. In the end, Adam gave up.

"Perhaps Will is right, and we can save a little."

Even though Adam said a speculative profit was not worth the risk, he reassured himself that all would become clear tomorrow.

Early in the morning, the phone rang. It was Will.

"Imagine that. I called Mr. Blum yesterday, and he said he would consider it. And now Allan said that the premises are already gone. This skunk, Blum, signed a contract with another tenant. That is a scam. Now we should pay Lev $1,125 each."

Adam hung up and did not say aloud what he thought about Will and his business method.

"Nata! You can't imagine what an idiot he is. I told him yesterday when he spoke to the guys about it. Due to the greed and stubbornness of that idiot, Will, we lost the premises and the money."

"It may be for the best," Nata replied thoughtfully. "The Komsomol Secretary, with his stupid ambition and self-confidence, could bring many problems to the business. So, $1,125 is a low price for the lesson."

"And you know, Nata, you're probably right. Maybe God saved me from getting into even worse troubles. That's it. I am finishing up this partnership. I'll pay Lev my share, and that's it. With these fools, it does not matter what business they are in. It is better to lose with a smart one than to find with a fool."

Montreal

ADAM HAD A FIRM INTENTION not to have any business partners but to do everything himself. He decided to take a break and temporarily leave his attempts to establish a business. Adam wanted to keep his promise to pamper Nata—and himself too. He had already gone a year without a vacation, working at Orsini's. Now Adam could afford to have a break. But beyond that, he had another old dream—to own a car.

A dealership that sold used cars was not far from their house. They went there to pick out an inexpensive car. Adam expected to spend about $3,000. He understood that a decent car was hard to find for that money, but it was worth trying. They found nothing for that amount as they walked across the parking lot. There wasn't anything decent. Finally, the manager came up to them. He politely smiled and, in a friendly tone, asked, "Can I help you?"

That standard phrase always left Nata in a stupor because of shyness or seeking natural protectiveness. She always hid behind Adam's back, leaving him to communicate with anyone who wanted to help.

"Yes, we are looking for a car, not expensive, somewhere around three thousand bucks."

"Any particular model? Year of release? Mileage?"

"No, we don't have such special wishes. We want a car that looks decent and doesn't have problems."

The manager focused on Adam and squinted. "You are from Russia? All great chess players are from Russia. And you surely play chess."

Adam was surprised at the transition to such a topic and shrugged. "I've played a little. But not often."

"I'm a Chess Club member and a huge chess fan." He enthusiastically introduced himself to his new acquaintance. "Do you live nearby? I'll bring chess tomorrow, and we must play with you."

"Ah, well. We can play a game or two."

"Wonderful! And by the way, I have a great car for you. Come, I'll show it to you."

Adam and Nata looked at each other, bewildered, barely holding back smiles, and followed behind this chess lover.

A selection of brilliant, dazzling, handsome sports cars was kept inside the dealership, where many cars were for sale. Adam squinted his eyes from the glitter of these exorbitant prices.

"Please, look at this dazzling Chevrolet Camaro—sports model. Jump in the seat. Look around; feel the spirit of this baby."

Adam and Nata sat back on the chic leather seats. It was a coupe, just for two. They couldn't simply sit in the car but almost lie down. Adam had never been inside a similar car; he had only seen them in movies. Wide sport tires spoke of speed and reliability. The long hood argued that the power of the engine was unlimited. Two huge wide doors opened almost one and a half meters out. The Chevrolet Camaro was the standard of speed and elegance.

"It seems I fell in love with it," whispered Nata.

"Yes, I did too. But, I'm afraid even to imagine how much it costs."

"For you, I'll give a special discount," said the strange salesman. "I can lower the price to six thousand. Do agree; it is almost a gift."

"The price is excellent, but we have only $3,000 and not a single cent more."

"That is not a problem. We will issue credit for half the cost, and you can pick up this beauty today."

Adam looked at Nata's happy face. They could buy the car if they took out a loan; it was not bad. He remembered the need for a good credit history, which he had hoped to build for a long time. To buy a car on credit was something substantial. They went in to do the paperwork to close the deal.

The salesman continued to use strange and even funny terms with Adam. He called his manager and persuaded him to offer a discount on a loan because the buyer knew how to play chess. This argument seemed ridiculous. Adam was sure the loan would be refused, but the salesman reported that the issue was resolved. The happy new owners of a chic car left the dealership, vowing to play chess with the salesman tomorrow.

Adam called Alex to boast about the new acquisition. They agreed to *"wash purchase up,"* an old Russian tradition, to drink on a new purchase. They agreed to meet on Sunday in Chinatown.

* * *

Capital of Immigrants

Adam and Nata had been in the area many times and liked it. Canal Street divided Chinatown in the south from Little Italy in the north.

Each of these areas was charming and unique in a different way. Chinatown contains many souvenir shops and restaurants. There were different food establishments, from tiny eateries with three tables to giant ones that easily sat a thousand people. Sales in Chinatown were effortless; on each side of the street, in shops, and generally any place, they would put out a cardboard box covered with newspaper, and the place could be ready for business. Chinese businesspeople started moving across Canal Street and buying property in the Italian section.

Little Italy was a contrast: a different atmosphere and very colorful. This part of town, which still survived, had huge crowds. The restaurants had outside tables full of happy customers. Busy cafés served drinks, coffee, and, of course, pasta.

In both areas, holiday festivities were often taking place. The Chinese New Year is celebrated with fireworks and colorful giant dragons moving through the streets, performing monster-flame dances. Italian carnivals were held where they served hot fried dough balls called *zeppoles* sprinkled with powdered sugar. Mandatory attributes of the feast were cannoli, Sicilian crispy rolls filled with cream, and many other national sweets.

New York generally had great street fairs. Event planners asked city officials to meet their demands; plans for the festivities required they close one street or another, sometimes even an entire avenue. That was also the procedure for national or religious holidays. Traditionally, the city's mayor, honorary citizens, celebrities, and many special guests would attend these events.

Whole columns of ships and platforms with wonderful and strange moving constructions hosted citizens who sang, danced, and modeled exotic costumes to celebrate such events.

Adam and Nata tried not to miss any. Even without carnival rides, they enjoyed Little Italy and Chinatown. Often, they met there with Alex and his family to have fun and good meals. The whole town came alive on such days, and this happiness seemed to be a pulse of New York. That Sunday, Adam and Nata came with the new car. Alex was indelibly impressed. He walked around the car and asked Adam, "Can I ride in it?"

He came back in half an hour. He was not himself from the storm of emotions.

He continuously kept saying, "I was lying in it! That is unthinkable! No, have you seen it? Here is the car. I was lying in it!" His wife, Nina, got tired of it.

"Calm down; yes, you were lying in it. We got it." Nina skeptically laughed and tried to bring her husband to common sense.

"Friends, let's go to the bar. My treat. A vodka martini should put your brains back in place," agreed Adam. "And then we'll have lunch in some Chinese restaurant."

"Only without clams." Alex frowned. "I remember we got it in *Roma di Notte.*"

"You don't understand. It was pasta *Frutti di Mare*," replied Adam.

"That was macaroni," said Alex. "I don't like these freaks with the macaroni."

Adam, unlike Alex, liked to try new things and share the joy of fresh impressions with friends. After drinks, they walked around Chinatown to a vast Chinese restaurant. Adam had already visited this restaurant with Nata, and now with

Capital of Immigrants

his knowledge, he enlightened Alex and Nina on traditional Chinese cuisine.

"We order different dishes—not for ourselves but for the table. We order a few substantial portions on the table. Then we can taste everything."

"Now, that's cool. Yes, Adam, do order for everyone. No clams, for God's sake."

They had egg drop soup and wonton soup with Chinese dumplings. The second round had a bowl of steaming-hot fried rice with shrimp and Peking duck. The meal was great, and they needed a break after it. In the Chinese tradition, in the end, everyone got a fortune cookie, a rolled, sweet cookie with a note inside of some written predictions. As always, these predictions were only optimistic. A little loosened up from a delicious dinner, Adam and Nata shared their plans for a mountain vacation. Alex and his wife supported their intention and envied such fortune.

The happy company decided to go to Little Italy for coffee and dessert. The cappuccino was superb for a warm summer night with a mild haze, and Adam thought this was only the beginning of their great life.

They crossed Canal Street and went to the main Italian street of this part of the town—Mulberry Street. Tables stood directly on the sidewalks. Everything was pleasant, as usual. Great coffee, traditional Italian desserts, and a lovely evening atmosphere.

* * *

The following day, Adam asked colleagues where he could go away for a week. Captain Mario remembered a hotel where he had vacationed with his wife and children. Mario gave Adam all the information. He immediately called Nata and reported the good news.

"We are going to the Catskill Mountains. The hotel is all-inclusive. We'll stay there for the whole week."

"Oh, how nice, Adam. I need to buy a dress. I have nothing to wear."

"Of course. Tomorrow we'll buy something for you."

The following day, they drove to Delancey Street. That was an old Jewish area on the Lower East Side in the past. In the 1980s, there still were many shops and small stores. Many small factories made all kinds of clothing and fabrics. They sold these garments to the small stores owned by immigrants, where they gladly greeted the immigrant buyers. They spoke an unimaginable mix of Yiddish and English; many still remembered Russian. Nata chose a dress that was too light of fabric and too theatrical for Adam's conservative taste. She believed this outfit was made for Cinderella magic and would wear it to the first ball. Adam didn't argue; he paid for the dress.

"Nata, since we're in this neighborhood, let's go to Katz's Delicatessen; we'll eat traditional and delicious pastrami sandwiches. Do you know they prepare the best pastrami sandwiches around New York?"

Nata had never tried pastrami. Adam told her, "Katz's has high-quality food. It's an old-time, well-known Jewish eatery. Many famous people, especially those who grew up on the Lower East Side, still come here. We will see a lot of old photos on the walls."

When they entered Katz's Delicatessen, they saw a new counter at the entrance. Behind it sat an older woman who took the customers' orders.

"Two pastrami sandwiches and a bottle of 7-Up."

She gave them two small tickets, and they went to the serving counter, behind which was a seemingly happy Russian guy in a white jacket. Adam handed him the tickets and put one dollar on the top.

The Russian gladly said, *"Spasibo"* (thank you) and shoved the money in his pocket.

He made the sandwiches and took two large rolls called "heroes" out of a warmer. The name came from "a hero," a serious eater, and flattering for the client. The sandwich was cut lengthwise and spread with mustard, and then the Russian guy pulled a sizable chunk of pastrami, a massive piece of juicy meat, out of the hot water. Deftly using a big fork and knife, he cut out long, thin slices and put them on the sandwiches. Then he added half-sour cucumbers and a bottle of soda.

"Preyatnogo appetite." (Good appetite.)

"Thanks." Adam took a tray, and they settled at a free table.

"Adam, why did you give him a dollar? Is it the tip? That is not a fancy restaurant."

"First, it's a tradition. Second, that's a good cut of meat from a lean piece, and he gave us a lot. You understand?"

"Wow, that's smart." Nata smiled.

* * *

The road to the Catskill Mountains was stunning. The car raced silently, quickly swallowing miles. In the 1970s, a national law was enacted, limiting the speed to fifty-five miles per hour. Crude oil prices multiplied because of the cartel agreement on "black gold." American scientists estimated that the most economical fuel consumption occurred when cars drove fifty-five miles per hour.

Police watched people and fined those going more than five miles per hour over the speed limit. However, most drivers violated this law. Adam drove at sixty-five miles per hour, sometimes going above ninety. The car quickly sped up, obedient to his commands. He felt almost no acceleration and would not know how fast he was going if he didn't look at the speedometer, and Na was afraid of fast speeds. Adam slowed down at her request but soon forgot and stepped on the gas again.

Drivers could not help but admire the car's beauty. The road ran along the wooded mountains covered with forests. The road was perfect and empty; passengers could not feel the hills.

"Wild mushrooms probably grow everywhere here," observed Adam. "Imagine, Nata, Americans do not collect wild mushrooms in the forest and will not eat them. They only eat champignons and white mushrooms from Italy called *porcinis*. Orsini's brought them frozen from Italy. I bought our Russian pickled white mushrooms in a glass jar for my boss. Do you know what he said? 'These are not Russian white mushrooms—they are Italian porcinis.' Hey, Nata, you're the navigator ... watch the map. Where are we? I do not want to miss our turn."

* * *

Capital of Immigrants

The room in the hotel turned out to be slightly small but comfortable. Adam opened the window. Children splashed and squealed in the pool in the middle of a big courtyard. They unpacked the suitcase, and Nata lovingly unfolded her new dress and hung it in the closet, planning to show it off in the evening.

"We'll go for a swim later when the children get tired," decided Adam. "Let's go check out the restaurant in the meantime. It's a strange system. What did the receptionist mention? Three meals a day on schedule, and in the evening, a disco? Snacks to order, but oh well. Hopefully, we will enjoy ourselveshere."

A youthful, smiling manager met them at the restaurant, and Adam asked about their dinner reservations, made in advance.

"You're two people? You will sit at table twelve."

He waved a hand toward a massive table for ten people.

"You see, my wife and I, this is the first time we have gone away, and we'd like to have something cozier. Is there a table for four people? It would be even better for two."

The manager pursed his lips. "We'll try to come up with something."

After a couple of hours, the swimming pool was still full of children; they had not dispersed, and they shouted and yelled so loudly that it hurt their ears, even in the room. So, Adam and Nata decided to walk to the disco hall, but it was locked. Dying hungry, they waited for lunch in their room to the accompaniment of TV and children's screams from the pool.

Later, when they headed to the restaurant, there was already a long line of senior citizens. When the door had barely opened, the retirees knocked on one another to be seated faster.

Nata and Adam looked for the manager, and he came with a strange smile.

"As you requested, something cozier."

Large tables sat in the vast dining hall for ten people, and their table, just for two, was clearly in the middle. People curiously looked at the table for two in the center of the room. It was a mockery.

Waiters brought trays full of thin glasses filled with fluid of a pale-pink color.

"What is this? An aperitif or maybe some juice?"

"Borscht! Cold beet soup!" voices rang out joyfully.

"Nata, did you hear that?" whispered Adam. " This dark liquid is an incredible surprise—borscht. What do we need to do with it, drink?

"Try a little bit. It's so delicious. True, the taste is slightly sour."

"No, thank you. I believe waitresses will now bring small cutlets with mashed potatoes, as we were fed in kindergarten."

Adam was right; it was mashed potatoes and cutlets. But the cutlets were made of carrots. He could not fathom it.

"It's a nightmare. We are trapped in a sanatorium for seniors with gastrointestinal tract diseases—a gang of elderly, soup-in-a-glass people eating carrot burgers. No, I can't stand a week here. I want meat, a vodka martini, and more optimistic talk than a kidney-stone discussion."

"Okay, Adam. Let's go to the store. At least you can buy meat and alcohol."

They set off on the path to the nearby village, but nothing was there. Walking outdoors made the couple even hungrier. They had to wait for dinner. Adam wanted to eat something juicy and familiar: a big sandwich with ham and cheese, even a sandwich with sausage.

Trying to escape from thinking about food, Adam suggested, "Let's go to the pool, shall we? Thank God; finally, there are no kids, and we can swim."

But the pool turned out to be closed. Furious, Adam read that the pool was only open until six in the evening. Adam felt that this was crazy. He went to the reception desk to find out why the pool was closed. The old lady looked quizzically at him as if he were outright stupid.

"You have to understand: people want to rest. The noise from the pool would disturb them."

"Fine, but what generally passes for fun in your institution for the elderly? That is not a hospital or a cemetery. Some guests want peas and carrots, while others want meat and fun. What then?"

"Well, after dinner, the disco will open. It will go on until twelve. And, by the way, there is a bar."

"Oh yes, what do you mean? Does it serve up something stronger than cold borscht?"

Adam confirmed that the dinner was healthy, and the disco was deserted and dark. A few elderly couples danced to the old, tedious, and melancholy music. Adam firmly decided that tomorrow morning, they would leave this hostel. There was no denying a lovely vacation—but for seniors.

"We are here thanks to Mario, who advised me to come here! Yes, that's it. I'll never, ever listen to someone's advice. Never in my life."

The following morning, Adam entered the reception area and demanded his money back for the week ahead. His ferocious appearance must have impressed the staff because, in fifteen minutes, the money was returned. Ten minutes after that, the Camaro carried two passengers racing toward Canada.

* * *

They decided to go to Montreal and stay in some hotel they wanted. They passed the border without stopping. Nobody whistled; the road was not blocked off with barriers. They were just able to enter the left side of the posts.

After an hour of driving, they crossed what seemed like a very long bridge, and the lights of Montreal flashed on the other side of the river.

"Adam, see that billboard advertisement? It seems like there will be a nice hotel up ahead. Look."

The King George Hotel was a grand, old-fashioned, and fabulous hotel. There were dance halls where balls probably had been given in former times. And there was a huge, old-fashioned bed.

"I'm afraid," said Nata, "that ghosts inhabit this place."

"Baby, what is there to fear? Look, there's a bible on the nightstand. It's just an old hotel. It's a little cool here. Yes, I will talk with the porter. And now let's go to the restaurant. I'm as hungry as a dog after carrot cutlets."

The restaurant was empty. An old waiter ceremonially led them to their table and invited them to choose something to drink.

"For me, a dry vodka martini, straight up. And for the lady, just ice water."

"You are from the United States?"

"Yes, from New York. Why? Is it so obvious?"

"You have an accent. Yes, and people don't order such drinks here."

Nata picked chicken, roasted on a grill, and Adam chose the Dover sole, a specially prepared fish the waiter brought on a big metal tray baked in the oven. He cleverly separated the fillets from the bones and put them on a plate in front of Adam using a fork and spoon. For the fish, Adam ordered a glass of cold Chablis.

The food was excellent; Adam finished with a coffee and a shot of Rémy Martin cognac. Nata preferred the ice cream.

* * *

They went to get acquainted with Montreal the following morning and had breakfast in a café. They ordered black coffee with milk and two buns, which they saw on the neighboring table.

The waitress corrected, "Those aren't buns; they are croissants."

The coffee was excellent, and they tried croissants for the first time.

"Adam, these are some delicious buns."

"It's not a bun; it's a croissant." He mocked the waitress, and Nata broke into laughter.

Montreal proved to be a wonderful city. It was a warm and pretty morning. There were numerous street cafés, crowds of tourists, and colorful surroundings. A brochure they read in the hotel said that Montreal was the capital of the French province of Quebec. And indeed, everything around it was metropolitan and French. There was unusual architecture, and the signs and conversations were in French. The stores were unlike those in the United States. Walking, they came upon a round kiosk advertising city tours and a panoramic night view of Montreal. It promised excitement. Adam bought two tickets for the bus tour, and they did not regret it.

At the end of the tour, the bus stopped at the site of Mont-Royal. The guide was also the driver, who loved the city and knew his work. He showed them all the finest buildings and landmarks; he talked about Montreal's past and present. Finally, the bus went to an open space, and the driver pointed out what he called a "little church on the hill." The people saw a gorgeous cathedral atop a high, radiant mountain. The view from the high mountain opened onto a magical, open-to-nature, magnificent view of Montreal.

"Such a wonderful place! Adam, can we come here again?"

"You can come again today, late evening," advised the bus driver. "We have night tours. I assure you, you won't regret it."

Returning to the tour kiosk, they bought tickets for the night outing. It turned out that it included sightseeing for dusk and evening lights, dinner in the restaurant, and visits to several nightclubs. Nata was slightly apprehensive, but Adam was so intrigued that he reluctantly agreed to a night adventure.

Dinner in the restaurant was excellent. First was an appetizer with a glass of white or red wine to choose from, and then the waiters brought paella. Adam tasted this dish for the first time, which impressed him so much that he would remember it forever. It was a fantastic dish, saffron rice, seafood, chicken, vegetables, and spices. It created a unique taste that he could not forget.

"Nata, you must try it. It's so unusual!"

Capital of Immigrants

But she was too shy to try new food, especially among an unfamiliar crowd. Then the tourists were taken to enjoy Montreal's nightlife. Adam had drunk a few glasses of wine with the fabulous paella and remembered only the Basilica of Notre Dame. He fell asleep and woke up only when the bus climbed Mont-Royal, and the top opened to beautiful night views of the city lights. Nata looked spellbound.

"Oh, Adam! It's such a magnificent view. Thank you."

The next stop was the cabaret Mont Parnas, where, according to the guide, there was "a gorgeous French striptease."

Nata blushed to the roots of her hair and wanted to stay on the bus.

Mont Parnas was a great cabaret. Tables with chairs descended to the stage by a theater, creating an excellent view. Guests were offered glasses of champagne.

The orchestra broke out, and a gaggle of partially naked maidens appeared on stage. Men welcomed that enthusiastically by whistling, shouting, and applauding. Nata got shy and turned her face away. Adam admired the beauty of the dancers. He was highly pleased with what they saw and entirely approved of everything that happened on stage.

This hot program ended at two in the morning. The tourists were then taken to a German pub. Smiling waitresses, dressed like those on beer festival posters, were carrying large glass mugs with foaming amber drinks. There were original wooden benches, capacious wooden tables, and hardwood floors. The stage was in the middle of the pub, where loggers in national clothes chopped a log with axes. Wood chips flew in all directions. The crowd sang, swinging to the beat. They danced, and some even jumped on a bench. Drunk and happy, Adam liked it all, and he tried to pull Nata up to dance, but she flatly refused.

The excursion ended early in the morning, and they woke up late the next day. However, there was nowhere to rush. Their greatest wish was to try French onion soup. Adam had long dreamed about it. They found a small restaurant with local cuisine. The soup was brought in clay pots with deep plates next to them. Solid chunks of bread and melted cheese floated in the pots. The dish was thick, rich, fragrant, and incomparably delicious.

"After such a soup, we don't need a second course," said Adam. "Montreal is a wonderful city. Maybe we'll move here."

"Adam, are you serious? I like it too. I like it here very much. I like everything."

"We'll think about it. First, we need to obtain American citizenship, but we can visit here as much as possible."

For the remaining days, they walked around and enjoyed the city. They roamed the Bonsecours Market, tried fried dough (simple fried pieces of dough with powdered sugar), and ate French crepes, the delicious pancakes made of buckwheat flour with stuffing.

That was so good. Strangely, in New York, there is no such fast food.

The week off, as always happened, was flying too fast. Even on vacation, Adam reviewed the information about his idea of fast food and pondered what business to open when they returned to New York. Nata and Adam sadly said goodbye to Montreal, having decided to visit there again.

The First Business

NATA SPENT HER DAYS DRAWING; it was her real passion. In Chinatown, they stumbled on a vast, fantastic shop. This building had once probably housed a factory or plant. All floors and stairs were made of iron, pipes, and fittings colorfully intertwined, and in this world of metal, people chose art supplies. The first floor was decorated with prepared canvases of various shapes and sizes. The second was occupied by shelving with various paints in cans, tubes, buckets, jars, and metal containers. There were albums for drawing and crayons in inconceivable colors. The third floor was for sculptors, where one could find accessories for this profession. And finally, on the fourth floor, there were things for artists who used sprays: costumes, masks, and huge cylinders with paint, in sizes from miniature to enormous.

Nata loved the long walks on each floor, and Adam typically tagged along, waiting for the end of a long shopping trip.

"Adam, can you imagine how this differs from what we had? When my parents' friends rode abroad, Mom and Dad implored them to bring good brushes and pencils. Dad joked that he would kill for a good brush. While at university, I did canvas linens for days, but I can buy them here, all prepared to draw. And look what is happening here. All the canvases are primed and available for paints, from watercolor to acrylic or oil. I can buy any paint in tubes if I want or in cans or bottles. Crazy shop! I want to buy something."

Buy whatever you want, and let's get away quickly."

Nata chose some brushes and paints. Moreover, she chose the brushes so carefully that it seemed like she was choosing jewels. Huge canvases barely fit in the trunk of the car. Now she drew all day, and Adam was happy that her tears were gone. True, the apartment had become like an artist's workshop.

One day the phone rang, and after much questioning, Adam realized that he had gotten some luggage sent from Russia more than two years ago before he got out of the country. He knew that Customs had opened the massive wooden box and searched it, as they generally did with anything that had been exported. He had forgotten about sending it from Russia with such hassle and disturbances.

Therefore, he hadn't put anything inside besides handicrafts, souvenirs, and a couple of Russian samovars to make tea. If Customs found something forbidden, perhaps he could be "immigrated" not to New York but somewhere over the Ural Mountains, where many prisons existed.

Adam ripped off this coffin of dampened, rough boards and pulled out souvenirs. He didn't know what to do with those things. To sell them was impossible. Okay, he could give some away as gifts. He could make a table for Nata's art supplies from the boards. He made such a table, and this ugly construction stayed in the apartment for some time.

Capital of Immigrants

Nata, like many young women, adored soft toys. Adam had once bought her a giant plush lion nearly her size. Another time, she persuaded Adam to buy two giant plush bears. One was white, and the other was brown. Adam had twice traveled by car to transport them. The bear was planted on the car seat next to the driver's, and people walked away in fear, likely thinking, *what the hell was the passenger in the car?* These animals had occupied much space in the room, and Adam often caught Nata in the company of plush friends.

The paintings, in Adam's opinion, were excellent. Nata loved painting as well as her toys. The subjects of the paintings were Russian folktales, and the pictures turned out bright, like the famous Russian lacquered Palekh handicrafts.

Adam thought that her talent could have some commercial success. Once, they even carried her work to the Museum of Modern Russian Art, which opened in New Jersey. But they took only abstract art and modernist paintings there rather than Russian folk art. Nata got very upset, and Adam scolded himself for convincing her to show her work. But the hopes of finding a way for Nata to succeed from her creativity had not left him.

One day, his eyes caught an advertisement about leasing space in the neighborhood near where they lived. In a small court was a mall with a few stores. A small space was available for an attractive price, just $500. He thought he might convince Nata to open a gallery.

"Honey, you draw all day, so why not try to capitalize on this? We will rent this room, and you will work directly in our gallery. We will place your paintings on the walls, and if we manage to sell at least one for five hundred dollars, it will cover the rent. Assume it's our first business. And who knows? Maybe your talent will get noticed by someone."

"No, Adam. I can't draw when someone is watching me."

"Let them look. Maybe someone will be interested in your art. For you, it's a great chance."

The next day Adam rented the space. He spent a long time trying to persuade her, and finally, she gave in. They brought her paintings and the two colossal plush bears. They connected a phone, and it became like an art gallery.

"Let's call it 'Two Bears Art Gallery,'" offered Adam. He printed small fliers and spread them all over, leaving them on car windshields and throwing them into mailboxes. Nata refused to draw in the gallery and dressed up to sit there all day. She chatted on the phone with her friends. His idea of showing the artist during the creative process didn't work out.

"Nata, we spent money on advertising, but they can't get through if anyone decides to call."

"I'm bored sitting here. And no customers have been here yet."

Adam already understood the plan failed but was too stubborn to give up. Once, a young man came through the door of the gallery. He examined the exhibited paintings and selected one.

"How much for this one?"

"This is five hundred dollars," Adam answered enthusiastically. "It is the work of the young artist ... very talented."

"Yes, I like it, and I'll take it."

Adam did not believe that he had finally sold a painting. That was the impetus for the decision to seriously engage in this business. The idea was that Nata would paint in the gallery in front of a curious public. But she steadfastly refused. Someone had finally bought one of her paintings so that it might work. The question was, could it work without an artist's presence? Ultimately, Adam asked Armando Orsini to let him go; he decided to devote himself to promoting the art store. But luck ran out, and his success left with the first buyer. Adam admitted his defeat at the second month of rent and closed the shop. He became scared that he would again have to go to the restaurant recruiting agency.

He could find a position in a decent place with a recommendation from a previous job. He called Orsini to ask Armando Orsini to give him a good testimonial. He was surprised when Signor Armando said, "Come back to us. You're a good bartender, Adam."

He was received with cheerful jokes and patted on his shoulder; no one gloated or rebuked. He was well accepted back into the team. It could happen to anyone. Adam was very grateful, especially to Signor Orsini. Life had only become routine, but Nata started to weep again daily. Adam thought that the reason was still the same—her parents—but it turned out that there was another reason. He was shocked by the event, which he had not seriously considered.

"I'm pregnant," Nata said through tears. "What will I do now?"
"I'm happy! We will get married and have a child; what else?"
"You seriously want that?"
"How can you be such a fool? Surely you didn't think I would throw you out. Your endless tears are because of this? Who do you take me for?"
"Sorry, I was afraid. I also said nothing to Mom and Dad."

"Call them now, and give them the great news."

Among the many things demanded from Adam were responsibility, commitment, and, most importantly, money. It was necessary to make an appointment for marriage registration and find a doctor to become their primary obstetrician. They had to buy the baby a stroller, crib, and many other things. Suddenly, they had a lot to do.

* * *

They met Adam's sister and her son John at the borough town hall, the only witnesses to the ceremony. Adam gave Sonya the wedding rings to hold. He filled out the necessary papers, and a tall, skinny African American man called them to the judge's office. In the room, there was not a soul. It turned out he was the judge. He monotonously muttered the words required. They signed papers and exchanged their rings. The newlyweds emerged from the office through another door. A big crowd waited for a turn to get married in the hall. Nata probably had dreamed about marriage "as it was supposed to be," with the wedding dress and the solemn celebration. But the reality for the immigrants was they lacked family members who could attend such events.

That narrowed the experience to a simple registration in a book of marriages rather than a ceremony. Adam promised himself that someday they would celebrate this day more sumptuously.

Cookbook

THEY WAITED FOR THE CHILD, and Nata had all sorts of fears. Adam thought about how to occupy Nata's mind. Since all of Adam's life was related to cooking, it was no surprise that he had the idea to write a cookbook. He bought a typewriter and learned to use it quickly, albeit with one finger. Nata had been involved in drawing; to Adam's delight, she was a magnificent artist.

The central theme of prerevolutionary Russian menus and recipes for dishes was chosen for his future masterpiece. Adam brought some old Russian cookbooks to America, published before the Bolshevik uprising. Such antiques were not easy to export; they required expertise and the official permission of the State Central Public Library. He had taken these books across many borders by paying the requested custom duty price and received the stamp on the books. Now, those books would help him make his very own creations. Adam got to work.

The manuscript turned out to be very attractive. He printed the text, and Nata did the illustrations. When the work was finished, it became clear that they should do something more.

Someone advised him, "Try to present the manuscript to the newspaper *New Americans*. The editor-in-chief, Sergei Dovlatov, is your compatriot ... maybe he can help."

* * *

A blonde secretary met Adam in the newspaper office with the familiar question. "Can I help you?"
Why do they ask that? Everywhere it's the same question. Sometimes I wish I could say in response, "Can you help financially?" It would be funny to see newcomer immigrants taking the stereotype at face value and telling the interlocutor their troubles and problems.
The blonde sent Adam to the deputy chief editor.
Adam got lost in the corridors until some Russian of an indeterminate age confronted him. He was very talkative and wanted to speak out. "Did you see all of this mess? I brought a business to them. I have come to pay for a promotional ad—I work and have money to give. I was sent from office to office. And neither the first nor the second is on-site. I went to the third, and he did not understand what I wanted from him. What's this newspaper? Is there someone leading this place?"
Two men were passing by. They went to some office behind a closed door, but voices were heard.
"How I'm tired of these shopkeepers. They are confused and underfoot with their petty problems, interfering with our work."
Adam's new acquaintance was choked by indignation.
"Did you hear him? That was Dovlatov. He names us shopkeepers! I brought him money. He was a correctional officer. And an alcoholic. Drinking like a pig."

Capital of Immigrants

"Okay, take it easy. Don't worry so much. And why 'correctional officer' and 'drinking'?"

"You don't know, eh? He was a security guard in the jail; he stood on the tower with a rifle. And why his drinking is understandable. Everyone knows that he is an alcoholic."

In the office of the deputy chief editor, several men argued and discussed operational issues. Adam waited a long time and wasn't getting any attention until he coughed.

"You—why are you here?"

After Adam explained, one man answered, "We could prepare the book for print. It costs $1,500. If you want to publish a small print run, it's another $1,500."

"And to sell?"

"That is your problem, man."

"It's clear. Let's do first a preparation to print."

Adam paid the money. He was taken to the book typesetter's office. There was a meeting he regretted afterward. There were two very cheerful companions. One was a fat guy called Peter, and the other was thin, Aleksandr. They smelled like an opened bottle of cheap wine. They worked in a small, dark studio, joked on any occasion, and quickly found common ground with Adam. The name on the book, *Forgotten Russian Cuisine*, delighted them. Both were very much lovers of tasty meals. The descriptions of the recipes, which were initially unfamiliar to them, led them to become big fans. They read the pages, savoring each recipe and asking if they were real. They read the text several times before going to typeset the book.

The text was printed on film and then glued to pages prepared for printing. Adam parted with Aleksandr and Peter as friends, and they wished him success.

Adam shared his joy with Nata at home—the book was ready for publication. He carefully removed the folder from a suitcase, hoping to print it at the first financial opportunity. What would be done after the publication? How would he sell it? Would he search for channels of distribution and advertising? Adam knew nothing about this business and decided to postpone it for a better time.

During these days, Adam had other projects. Years later, he learned that Peter and Aleksandr were clever, and the bold, jolly fellows published his book under their names. In the United States, the collection of recipes for Russian cuisine had no success, but it was successful in Russia.

One day, as Adam drove his car, he heard an interview live on Russian radio with the famous two fellows thanks to his book. His anger and rage boiled so that he almost got into an accident. His first instinct was to call the radio station and publicly expose the scam. But then what would he get? He would blow off steam, and then what? What is the point of exposing them? He could go to court to prove his authorship; he could benefit from drafts and preserve the source text. He could punish the plagiarists and seek compensation. The money, however, would be peanuts. Was the moral satisfaction worth all the hassle, cost, and bureaucratic effort to restore justice? Adam long pondered what to do. Ultimately, he decided that the most sensible thing to do would be to forget it. The whole story smelled terrible, and he felt nasty and dirty from those fellows. They would not have earned anything without his work. God would see the truth.

When he worked with another publisher on a new book many years later, Adam told him about this painful experience. He was surprised when the publisher, with round eyes, pulled the same cookbook off the shelf.

"Adam, they made names for themselves on this book. You gave it to them. What are you going to do? I am ready to help you restore justice."

"I don't know. So much time has passed. I will consult with my wife. Someday I'll write a story about those crooks. Let us not forget: one of the Ten Commandments says, 'Thou shalt not steal.'"

Christmas Baby

NATA'S PREGNANCY PROCEEDED FINE, expecting childbirth at the end of the year. There was still plenty of time to buy all the essentials before the baby's birth. They often went for a ride in Manhattan, usually getting stuck in heavy traffic. That happened quite often. But one time, Nata suddenly fell in pain. Adam tried to move the car out of the traffic, but all the avenues and streets behind him were blocked. He started to honk, demanding other drivers give way, and a police officer came over.

"Officer, my wife is pregnant, and she feels sick. Please help me get out of here on any side street. We urgently need to go to the hospital."

"Why did you honk? Don't you know that this is prohibited?"

"Yes, of course, I know. I'm sorry, but you can see that we have a big problem."

"And so, with your behavior on the road, you decide to create a problem for everyone?" asked the policeman sarcastically.

Adam thought he had misheard. Who knew how the conversation would have ended if Nata had not intervened. Breathlessly, she moaned from either pain or anger. "Officer, why should we care about your problems if you don't care about ours?"

The policeman was dumbfounded. He pursed his lips and began to issue a fine.

Adam yelled, "Officer, help us, please! What are you, blind? My wife is about to get very ill. We must be admitted to the hospital urgently."

The policeman squinted doubtfully at him and Nata, wavering, but he eventually helped clear the path for the vehicle. Finally, they drove to a free street. The hospital was a few blocks away, and they got there quickly. The doctor on duty examined the patient and prescribed soothing drops.

"Don't worry. All is well with the child. Your wife is slightly frightened, but soon the medication will work, and you can go home in half an hour."

The police officer appeared at the hospital.

Probably worried, too, was Adam's thought.

But he handed Adam a copy of a fine notice and arrogantly explained, "If you do not agree, then I've written the date to appear in court and contest the violation."

The policeman disappeared. Sitting in a wheelchair, Nata guiltily looked at Adam, but he was afraid she would worry and get worse, so he silently swallowed this offense.

"Do not pay attention, honey. I will go to the court and explain everything. This nasty bastard should answer."

* * *

Adam described the situation at the hearing, ensuring the judge could not be indifferent and unfair as the policeman. He ended his speech by describing how the policeman put the fine note directly on Nata's hospital bed.

The judge adjusted his glasses and asked, "He just went ahead and put it on the bed in the hospital?"

"Yes, Your Honor."

"Mmm ... yes. Well, it happens. Go to the cashier, pay the fine, and you are free."

"I—what?"

"The next case is ..." The judge was already busy again.

Adam walked out of the courthouse feeling that someone was having a good laugh at his expense. At home, he did not tell Nata anything. It was frustrating, yet he was worried about disturbing her with another manifestation of human injustice and indifference.

* * *

Halloween, a favorite holiday for American kids, approached. Adam bought a lot of candies and sweets to treat the children, who, as usual, went from apartment to apartment and rang the doorbells.

"Trick or treat!"

Dressed in scary costumes and excited, the children were screaming with laughter. They filled small bags with sweets; sometimes, people gave nice little things, and everybody was happy. But most importantly, Nata was having even more fun than the kids, making Adam happy.

Then there was Thanksgiving Day, an important holiday for Americans.

Christmas and Thanksgiving were considered the most important family celebrations, and Nata and Adam liked this tradition when the families got together.

There was roasted turkey with cranberry sauce, sweet potatoes, and pumpkin pie. Unfortunately, Nata's parents could not share this joy with them, but as part of their Thanksgiving Day culinary masterpiece, the table was full of Native American gifts.

Adam bought a small turkey and cooked it in the oven, following the instructions on the packaging. The bird proved amazingly soft and delicious, and the pumpkin pie they had for the first time in their lives was also excellent. The Christmas season started after Thanksgiving Day. The whole country purchased and prepared gifts for Christmas night. Gifts were placed under Christmas trees. Children and adults wrote letters to Santa Claus, hoping their dreams would come true. New York was decorated with multicolored electric lights, figurines, garlands, and wreaths. On the doors of houses and apartments popped green wreaths, which led immigrants from Russia to make many jokes; wreaths were associated with funeral traditions in their abandoned homeland.

Immigrants celebrating the first holiday season in their new homeland were not financially stable, so they usually waited for December 26. The New Year celebration remained the main holiday for Russians, including Adam and Nata. On this day, strange Americans sometimes throw Christmas trees in the trash and could be with decorations. It seemed wild, especially in contrast with Russians usually keeping their trees sometimes until the end of winter.

That year, Adam and Nata were preparing for the New Year holidays and the birth of their child. The union would pay most childbirth expenses but still have to pay for many things themselves. Nata often visited the doctor, and Adam worked a lot, saving for future expenses.

On Christmas Eve, everything was closed, and no one worked; it was accepted in the West. Adam and Nata weren't going anywhere to celebrate this holiday that was new to them. Late at night, Nata felt terrible, and it became clear: her labor had started. Adam gently put her in the elevator, and they got in the car.

Adam had thought many times about how this day would be. He was mentally prepared for the responsible moment. But his hands shook with fear when Nata moaned from the excruciating pain. Adam was speeding in the car and asked God, "Just let me get there—just help, please."

At the hospital, he raced for help. A whole group of medical personnel with stretchers ran out, and they rushed Nata inside. Adam parked the car and went inside to find his wife moaning even harder. Nata was in great pain.

"My contractions are coming even more often. They called our doctor; he will come soon. But they said to wait until the contractions are continuous. Won't you leave me alone? I am terrified, Adam."

"Of course, no! I'm not going away. I'm with you."

"Hello, hello." The doctor entered the room and smiled. "Hello, darling, you picked a great day to give birth. Right at Christmas."

"Sorry, Doctor. I didn't want to spoil the holiday for you."

"Nata, this day is good. It's a blessing from God to be born on this day. We call such kids 'Christmas babies.' Let's check to see how we are getting on. It looks as though there is still time.

I shall pray for good delivery and advise you to do the same. Adam, here is a chapel for worshippers."

"No, thank you, Doctor. I'd rather be here with my wife."

Nata prayed. Adam would have done so himself, but he didn't know how. The contractions became more frequent. Nata was covered with droplets of sweat, and she didn't stop moaning and screaming. He could see that it was unbearably painful. Adam feared that something terrible and irreparable would happen before his eyes, and he would not be able to do anything to help. He was losing his mind from this inconceivable anguish, and Nata's growls were like an animal in nature. After the doctor came, everything was moved to another room. Surrounded by numerous medical staff, Adam held Nata's hand and tried to breathe correctly with her as they had been taught in the prenatal classes. But neither he nor Nata could do it properly, and Adam seemed to have forgotten how to breathe. He lost his sense of time and didn't realize who the doctors were and what was happening. It was an eternity, and his brain refused to understand how Nata survived this nightmare.

Suddenly, someone loudly said, "It's a girl!"

What girl? Where is the girl? Who lets a child in here?

With dull eyes, Adam looked around, expecting to see a girl with bows in the room.

It made sense only when the doctor explained, "Congratulations, you have a daughter!"

He looked at her tiny red and wrinkled face and blurted out, "*Baba.*"

That, in the simple Russian language, meant "woman." He looked at Nata's weary face, the wrapped bundle, and tears rolled down his face. He wasn't thinking; instead, he didn't understand what he had said and what had happened.

The nurse took the child, and Nata was rolled to the postnatal room. Adam was walking nearby, and all that had happened seemed unreal. He could not believe that the worst was behind them. Nata quietly fell asleep, exhausted but happy.

"Go home; sleep too. And in the morning, come back," advised the doctor.

"And nothing will happen to them?"

"She and the baby will have a long sleep. They are worn out, poor things."

Adam returned home and, without undressing, collapsed onto the bed. In the morning, he jumped up, horrified. Sticky fear grabbed him by the throat, and it did not go until he saw his girls. Nata nursed the child, and an indescribable smile covered her face. The baby had closed her eyes and smacked her little lips; the biblical picture was unspeakably beautiful.

"I'll go to buy you a meal and come back," whispered Adam. "What do you want?"

Nata only blissfully shook her head.

Adam found the nearest outdoor store and got all he could think of and find. When he returned to the hospital, he saw his sister, Sonya, in the hall.

"Congratulations, Daddy! You have a daughter! Can I look?"

"Let's go to the nursing room."

They approached the large glass wall. From there, they could see transparent boxes with sleeping newborns.

"And where is yours?"

"Right here. In the second row ... the one on the right."

Capital of Immigrants

"And how did you know? They all look the same; you cannot distinguish them from one another."

But he had learned her face immediately. Nadia was different from other kids. There was his Nadia. Adam and Nata had long argued about the name for a boy, but the one name for the girl they had chosen immediately—Nadia. It meant *hope* in Russian. Adam realized that from now on, Christmas would be his favorite holiday.

After a couple of days, Nata was discharged from the hospital and was advised to see a pediatrician. It was recommended that they consult the office of Dr. Bass and Dr. Beer. Adam made fun of their names.

"Oh, wow, Dr. Bass and Dr. Beer! Strange and inappropriate for babies' doctors."

Once, Nata told the pediatricians how they treated children with colds or sore throats in Russia. But they were doctors from God. They taught the new parents how to feed the baby, swaddle her, and bathe her, and they explained the many vital details and nuances about the baby, which the young parents had no idea about.

"In Russia, if children cough, we give them eggnog or warm milk with honey."

The doctor thought and seriously asked, "And the children improve after this? Mucus has already formed; if you give them warm milk, it adds to the mucus."

"What about you, Doctor? So how do you treat them?"

"It is better to give something cool. A piece of ice."

There were dozens of pieces of advice like this, and they truly benefitted from them.

In the meantime, there was shocking news from Moscow. In recent months, Nata's mother had felt worse and worse. She apparently could not accept that the Soviet government had condemned her to eternal separation from her daughter and now her granddaughter. She gradually faded away and died. Nata experienced the loss very heavily. Secretly she had hoped that their reunion would come about sooner or later, but now all that remained was her dream that her father would be able to get out of the USSR. He filed documents for departure again and again but was repeatedly denied.

Because of these events, Nata lost her breast milk and could not feed the baby. They began to use ready-made infant formula. In addition, Nadia usually did not fall asleep quickly, and Adam had to rock her in her baby car seat.

It was the only way to put her to sleep. Adam himself became exhausted, and for the first time after the birth of his daughter, it was a real test for him. He often fell asleep at work, but realizing that the family's financial well-being depended on him, he regularly made it to Orsini's. Thoughts about their own business huddled on the periphery of his consciousness. He was responsible for two people and now had no right to undertake such adventures.

Time for Change

THERE WAS NEVER A LACK of risky situations in life. Over the winter, their chic Chevrolet already had three problems, and Adam thought something was wrong with this car. The first problem started with some crazy car racer who shattered Adam's car's rear wing. It left a severe dent, and the driver sped away. There were neither witnesses nor police, and the driver had gone with such speed that Adam could not recall the car's color or brand. The family had been in the car, planning to walk into Chinatown. Both of them were scared. The child was sleeping and didn't even wake up. Adam had to make a decision.

"We will go to Manhattan and park our car. Then we'll go for a walk, as we were going to, and then go back and find traces of the accident. Maybe the police can then figure out who hit us and ran."

"Adam, it's terrifying. What if they couldn't uncover who it was?"

"What can we do now? Stand on the highway and wait until someone comes? There were no witnesses to the incident."

"Adam, you have iron nerves."

"I don't see any other options for protecting our interests."

They drove to an empty parking lot. They left the car, pulled out the stroller, and walked on Canal Street. It was Sunday, and Chinatown was full of people. Adam pondered how the police would start looking for the bad guys. They probably would send investigators to inspect the accident scene and determine the color of the other car involved in the collision. And then there would be an investigation.

But it turned out to be simple. The officer on duty at the police station asked where they went and asked for their car documents. He established the protocol and gave Adam the case number. Then he yawned and explained, "Call your insurance company and give them this case number. They know what to do."

"And that's it? Nothing more? Hmm, you will not do anything?"

"What can we do? Put the whole police department on alert? Yours was a typical car accident; it happens every minute."

At home, Adam called the insurance company and dictated the case number.

They promised to send a specialist to take photos of the damage to the car. After a week, he received a check for $800.

The rear wing of the Chevrolet was unlucky. Adam did not have time to use the compensation money he received for repairs from the insurance company. Soon after, the car was hit again by another car in the same rear wing. The procedure was the same, with two exceptions: the offender did not escape from the crash site this time, and the insurance company sent another check for $1,100.

Something does not please God with this car. I have to sell it.

But fate decided by itself, and it could not have been better. A couple of days later, Adam didn't find the Chevrolet where he had left it in the morning. At the police station, the officer looked at him with suspicion. Nevertheless, Adam was given a case number relating to the car theft, which he dictated to his insurance company over the phone. Soon, Adam received notification that the insurance company had paid off the car loan. In addition, he received $500 from the bank for paying the loan ahead of time.

"Nata, see how insurance worked. We can now buy a new car. I think we can do it in Pennsylvania. Someone wrote an ad about a huge used-car market in a Russian newspaper. So, it will be cheaper and better. Plus, from there, it will be transferred for free."

He called the number in the ad and arranged a trip the following week. In the morning, a driver came to pick up Adam. There was another man who also wanted to buy a car. The driver told them how it worked.

"In Pennsylvania, there is a massive market of thousands, if not tens of thousands, of secondhand cars for sale, but not many buyers. I work for a dealer and bring some interested clients. There's a challenge, and the price is lower than in New York. The cars are mainly used on highways, so they are better than in New York. They are in perfect condition because people living there are mostly rich and accustomed to replacing cars every three years. Thus, everyone benefits: the buyer receives a decent car for a competitive price, the car dealer sells goods, and I get income as a mediator and a cabby."

They were at the place two hours later and began circling the car dealers' sites and inspecting the cars. Adam noticed a black Mercedes 200 SE from afar; it was love at first sight.

This car was a dream. It had a black lacquer coating, flare sides, and a wide chrome grille. The Mercedes looked embarrassingly expensive and noble. All in all, it was very tempting, and Adam was hoping for a successful purchase.

"How much do you want for this?" Naïve, Adam asked casually, struggling not to show he had fallen in love with this car.

"Yes, first, see if you like it. Take it for a test drive. I'm ready to give it to you for five thousand."

Adam had only three, and he did not want to spend more. The negotiation was crazy until the seller dropped the bottom bracket to four thousand.

"Look, I believe you have only $3000, and I'm ready to accept it. I will give you the car now. But you send me a check for a thousand when you arrive home."

"Are you sure you can?" Adam was surprised. "And if I cheat?"

"Not a problem. I'll keep the title. Without it, you will not be able to register it. I'll give you transit numbers; they are good for thirty days. You call your insurance company and get the car insured right now. Well, is it a deal?"

Adam, still sluggish, resisted, but they knew the transaction had already occurred.

Getting home, Adam left the car in the underground garage of the house with the keys in the lock. Those were the rules, and violating them meant residents lost the use of the garage. He excitedly told Nata about the purchase and how he had succumbed to the black chrome German beauty.

Nata, as always, had little interest in value, credit, and other financial issues and exclaimed, "Oh, I want to see it! Let's go for a ride."

They went down to the garage, but the car wasn't there.

"Where is my Mercedes?" Adam was frightened and ran to the garage security.

"You have a Mercedes?" The guard was genuinely surprised.

"Yes! Today, I bought it. And five minutes ago, I left it here."

"Oh, so this is yours. I have it at the end of the parking lot; I drove it away from trouble. If such a German car gets any scratches, there are many problems. These kinds of cars have expensive repairs."

When someone bought a used car, it was well known that it should be scheduled for a comprehensive service. Very soon, Adam personally saw why. Adam drove the car to a station that specialized in Mercedes. When he got the bill, it was a shock. The employees only shrugged.

"Man, Mercedes are iron on wheels. To maintain such a car, you must earn good money. This car is good for lawyers or doctors."

Adam realized what a silly mistake he had made. He could not afford this car. He needed to sell and replace it with something more reasonable and practical.

* * *

Life went on as usual, and Alex called one evening.

"Hi, Adam! Here is the thing: two guys are selling a business in Brooklyn, a car service. Did you ever hear of this?"

"Something connected with taxis?"

"Not quite. The yellow cabs with medallions mean licenses. One medallion is worth thirty-five thousand bucks today. There are more than eleven thousand medallions in New York, and all work in Manhattan. Nobody wants to go to Brooklyn or Queens because their return is always empty, losing money and time. Car services serve these areas. People need this service because they must ride to the hospitals, pick up airport guests, etc."

"Alex, what do we have to do with it?"

"Some guys are selling a popular car service with a list of customers and a well-advertised telephone number. We ought to go there to see, to check how everything works. It costs over fifteen thousand, and bargaining is not appropriate. Then we could think of what to do."

"We can go there and look; it's not a problem. But what is the point? To buy a business is a different story. Money is a problem now. I only have $4,500 on hand. I'm stuck with selling my Mercedes; plus, I must consider my baby. Every month we spend a certain amount on the child."

"I will add as much as you need. You can pay me back from the profit. Oh, come on, let's meet tomorrow."

* * *

The car-service office was in Brooklyn, in the Bensonhurst neighborhood, where most middle-class Italians lived. Not so long ago, Russians started to immigrate to the US. New people in America were not distinguished by nationality. They were called Russian, whether they were from Georgia or Ukraine. Alex and Adam had no idea what risk was involved in entering someone else's territory.

The office consisted of only a tiny room, which was leased. An old wooden partition divided the desk, and there were a few chairs up front for drivers. The most valuable core value item was the phone number and the client list. It was not the business unit itself; it had invested significant funds to become known to clients. The main competitive feature of this car service was the charge for a local call for a ride: $1.75. The other services had charged two dollars. The car service operated seven days a week from early morning until late. The owners were Mark and Serge, who referred to themselves as "two young boys." They firmly stood their ground and would not make concessions to buyers.

"Want to check out the business? Deposit the amount of 30 percent of the value. If you do not confirm what we told you about our business after a week, take back the money."

"And if it is confirmed?" Adam was worried.

"Then pay the remaining portion, and the business is yours."

"But if we change our minds?" continued Adam.

"The deposit remains with us."

Adam and Alex went to discuss it on the street. To Adam, it seemed like the Sizzler experience all over again. There were similar schemes and no guarantees. Furthermore, he had sworn he would say no to business partners and do everything himself. But here was another story. That was the same Alex whom he had known for many years. How much vodka had they drunk together? There were many years of friendship.

"Adam, we have nothing to lose. If the business makes money, we will take what they said as truth.

We will check it here for a week and learn how it works from the inside out. If there is a problem, we will find it and get our money back. All the expenses are included: the monthly telephone and office rent is $300. It should be resolved now because someone could still be offering more money for it."

"Yes, it all sounds tempting, but it's the same scenario; I have no right to risk the well-being of my family. I have a child, and I must bring home money no matter what. If I leave Orsini's again, they will not take me back. So, I'll talk with my wife and then call you."

He went home in doubt. It was clear that Nata, in such matters, was not a good adviser. He must take responsibility for everything just because he is a man. He did not intend to shift the responsibility onto a woman's shoulders, although it would be easier if she said no.

Adam painfully weighed the pros and cons. He feared he would stupidly jeopardize Nadia's future; this was the main argument against taking the risk. But he knew what the future would hold if he continued to work for someone else.

The worst thing that could happen is failure and money loss. Well, it would mean that I would be in bondage again. I can always get hired as an employee and work as before.

He decided it would be wise to take a risk.

Partners

THE COMPANIONS MET before entering their future office.

"Alex, let's discuss everything again. This week we will check the business from morning till night. Those guys sing well, but their mission is to sell the business. So, we need to check it all out. I can be in the office in the morning and afternoon, and you can come in the evening. When everything is in order, we will give them the money. I need to borrow three thousand dollars from you and pay you back over six months."

"Well, okay, Adam. How many times can you repeat the same thing? Let's go."

The owners were already waiting for them. When they finished the formalities, Alex and Adam gave them the $5,000 security deposit. The owners explained to them the everyday routine in the car-service business. Everything was clear and understandable except for one thing.

"Tell us, guys, why don't you insure the drivers and vehicles?" Adam asked when he heard about it.

"This is the drivers' concern, not ours. Everyone must have insurance; if they get in an accident, they must work with their insurance companies."

"And what about taxes?"

"What taxes, man? That is a small personal business. Do you wish to get all clean and legal and bring a nice profit for only $15,000? Come on."

"And if there is an accident?"

"Then we tell the passenger to deal with the driver. The driver does not work with us. We do not know who he is. It's the very first time we've seen him. Okay, it's time to start, guys. Calls from customers soon will begin."

The new prospective car service owners prepared for work, and Alex, revealing how he was worried by Adam's questions, whispered, "Adam, don't be foolish. First, we'll figure out what's what, make a little money, and then think about how to do it right. Come on."

"I need to go to work," Adam looked at his watch. "My shift starts at the restaurant soon. You stay and write everything in a notebook. Most importantly, count the incoming calls, and check the daily revenue. These two fellows can add to the book whatever they want; we are only buying the phone number." Adam was driving to work and thought about the new venture and what would happen.

This "black" scheme with taxes and no insurance is not suitable. Still, on the other hand, many small businesses live and struggle the same way in New York. It is necessary to warn at work that I might have to quit Orsini's. Then I should look for new housing; driving from Queens to Brooklyn daily is too far. I also have to sell the Mercedes and buy a substantial car. And all this might have to be done within a week.

* * *

Capital of Immigrants

The next day in the office, Adam met an excited Alex.

"Hey, yesterday I checked inside and out. Everything is great. We can take the business. I even made one call myself."

He was animated.

"Alex, you're not supposed to go anywhere. Your task was to sit and take calls and collect the money. Our fellows could have altered the bookkeeping to any numbers."

"Yes, Adam, I understand. But a call came in, and there were no drivers. They all were on calls, and what could I do? Well, I went, but now I will go no more. Don't panic. What about your work? Did you tell your boss you are leaving?"

* * *

Signor Armando Orsini had shaken his head and wished Adam good luck.

"You're a brave man, Adam Gardov. In one case, you left to write a cookbook, then opened an art gallery, and now, you are going into the transport business. I wish you success. I am sorry to say goodbye to a good bartender."

Adam also said many nice things in response to Orsini that he sincerely meant.

Adam was very attached to those Italian guys at work. They had taught him to drink wine and swear in Italian. They showed him respect and taught him to love family values. This work linked their strong ties. These guys shared sincere wishes of luck with him.

The partners checked the business through the end of the week. All promises were confirmed. This week's profit had been good, and the car service worked as was said. So, the agreement was signed, and the money was paid. They said goodbye to the former owners.

Adam asked, "Guys, honestly. Is there something we better know before it happens?"

It was understood; there was something. The previous owners looked away.

"Well, actually, there was something. From the beginning, we have had problems with locals. That is their territory, the Italians. The Russians had just started to settle here. In general, the Italians started first, but we worked this out, and now, everything is in order. I think you have nothing to fear."

"Well, how did you work it out? If it is not a secret?"

"In the Brighton Beach area, Evsey, the godfather, is a guy. He's from your city, Leningrad. He looks after the Brighton Beach area. Someone said he has electro-shocker sticks used for livestock. This Evsey sent his man, who stayed in the office for a few days. Everything worked out fine."

"And how much did it cost you?"

"It doesn't matter now. You won't need it. There are no more problems. But if something happens, you know what to do. I'm sure you won't have any collisions."

Things did not go as smoothly as the former car service owners promised. On the first day, all drivers were dispatched on orders, and even Alex had gone on a call; Adam sat in the office and answered calls. There was a lot of work, and he did not immediately notice that a stocky, muscular guy had appeared in the office.

"Are you the new owner of this business?"

Capital of Immigrants

Adam nodded.

"Hi, I'm Michael. My father owns the movie theater and other businesses on this street. And you, as you said, are the new owner of the car service? Yes? Good. Before, you could not have had a business here. It's our Italian territory. Do you like baseball?"

Adam didn't understand the connection to the sport.

"But you know baseball players, and they're not the only ones who use baseball bats?" Now Adam understood.

"Michael, my name is Adam Gardov. I am glad to get acquainted. Look, it's elementary: I came here to build a business. I don't want to fight for territory. Previously I worked in a restaurant called Orsini's in Manhattan. Have you heard of this place? I am familiar with Armando and his brother, Guido, and, indeed, with all the guys from there. I have an excellent relationship with them. So hopefully, we can come to reason."

Michael looked at him, evaluating, and changed the course.

"About the baseball, it was a joke. With prior boys, we got acquainted and even played cards. Do you mind if we assemble here sometime? You do play cards?"

"I'm not a fan of it, but you're welcome if it does not interfere with the business."

"I'm glad we understand each other." Michael winked and retired.

When Alex returned, Adam told him about his conversation, but Alex didn't even have time to wonder or ask questions. A hefty man of incredible proportions came into the office.

"Hi, guys; I'm Dima. And you seem to be the new owners. Did the boys who were here earlier tell you about me?"

Of course, they didn't tell us a name, but it is so apparent with you, thought Adam.

"Dima, hello. I'm Adam, and this is my partner, Alex. You're right on time. Michael, the leader of this block, has just now gone. We agreed on everything with him. But we know where to look for you if something is wrong."

"Well, guys, do you mind if I stay with you today?"

"Not a problem. Do you want some tea?"

The day passed quietly, and in the evening, Dima left, leaving his phone number in case something happened; they should immediately let him know.

* * *

Adam's family's housing had to be changed to an apartment in the Bensonhurst neighborhood. Of course, it was not Forest Hills, but compared to the old studio in Queens, they could afford a "royal" apartment: parking space, a hallway, a dining room with a kitchenette, and a separate bedroom.

They needed to solve the problem with the child's doctor; a ride to the other end of town to Dr. Bass and Dr. Beer was too uncomfortable. Adam promised Nata he would solve this issue. Nata was satisfied. One of the drivers, Boris, did help Adam to move to the new apartment. He flatly refused to take money.

During the housewarming party, Boris and Adam pondered over a bottle, discussing the fate of immigrant drivers and the transport business in general.

"Listen, Adam. I'm sorry, but I'll tell you straight: people who enter the car service because they cannot get decent jobs.

Capital of Immigrants

Everyone has different reasons. Some have language problems; some older men want to help the family; others might be simply unlucky, like me. My brother had already bought a fuel truck. He sells gasoline to the stations and makes great money. He called me, too, but I'm afraid."

"Why are you afraid? He does not carry stolen gasoline."

"That's the thing. On Brighton Beach, many people are involved in this topic. People buy gas stations and fuel trucks. A barge with gasoline comes somewhere in New Jersey, but that is not legal. No one pays taxes. The gasoline is drained, and cash is paid for fuel. I fear for my brother. They're already shooting at each other over there."

"If everything is as you say, the cops will soon begin to arrest them. You are right to be afraid and stay away from this."

* * *

Soon, as the Americans said, an event showed *who is who*.

Adam stopped at the stationery shop and bought the necessary things for work: pens, pencils, erasers, and a thick notebook for accounting. The total was $16.50. He entered the office and told Alex, "That's every little thing I bought. There was a discount, so I saved a little. We've been writing on small paper with small pencils in the office. Now we will be much better. I'll take money from the cash register, and you write it for general expenses."

"You know, Adam, it's all for you. You bought this stuff. You paid, and this is now yours. I'm quite satisfied with what we already have."

Angry, Adam went outside, feeling that he couldn't help thinking about the greed and pettiness of his companion. He had previously noticed that Alex was sometimes a miser, but to be so cheap and to such an extent? They had invested $15,000 in this joint business. How could they save money on such necessary costs as pencils and paper?

Maybe purchasing pens and pencils became an occasion to let off steam. Adam thought that maybe Alex was just upset about family problems or something else for a moment. If it were so, then he would come to his senses. Alex would apologize, and they would still be friends and laugh at this story.

But no one laughed. Alex never thought of asking for forgiveness. Moreover, there was something incomprehensible about this quite stupid situation. Adam worked as a dispatcher for two days, and Alex didn't even appear at the office. He finally came on the third day, but they didn't speak.

To be in the same room was impossible. Tension was in the air, and even the drivers who were subordinate to them felt it. Adam was the first one to speak. He announced, not explicitly addressing anyone, that he was going to Pennsylvania to change his Mercedes for a different car. Alex didn't react.

In Pennsylvania, all went smoothly. Adam returned to New York with a Dodge, a four-door sedan with a powerful motor. That was what he needed to work in the car service. Plus, he brought back $1,500 as the difference in the cost of the cars. The drivers rated the Dodge in the office and approvingly nodded their heads. Only one of them had experience working with reselling used cars.

"It does not look modern. What are those forms?"

"Form is only important when looking at women; I need the car for work. The main thing is that it's powerful."

Alex sat behind a partition and didn't participate in the conversation.

* * *

At home, Adam told Nata about the recent developments and added, "I need to do something about it. I won't be working with this cheap idiot. The problem is our money is in this business. I owe $3,000 to this idiot. I won't go back to Orsini's. I can't work during Alex's shift, and I have to look for work in other car services. We need to get out of this hole."

But finding additional work turned out not to be so simple.

Brooklyn car services needed drivers, but they needed someone to work daily. Others had two or three company cars, and all orders were given to them first. Some preferred to hire only their fellow compatriots from Odessa. The situation seemed to be a stalemate, and the relationship between Alex and Adam worsened. One day, one of the former owners of the business, Serge, popped into the office.

Alone with Adam, he asked, "I heard you have a problem with Alex. What happened? Did a black cat run between the two of you?"

Adam unexpectedly told him all about what happened.

"Yes, that happens sometimes; that is all a typical Brooklyn story. I always wanted to leave it and do business in Manhattan.

There everything is different, the people and money. Listen, maybe we each put in five big ones and open a car-and-limousine service in Manhattan. I know guys with limousines ready to transport; they are looking for work. I'm ready to fit in; if you can pull out your money."

That was the solution, but Adam didn't know how to resolve it. Alex, all of a sudden, offered the way out. Perhaps he had also reflected on the current situation and wanted to get out of this partnership. On Adam's shift, he appeared at the car service.

"It looks like our relationship isn't working out," started Alex. "What's happened, happened. I have someone who will buy your share, and we will disperse. For you, this business is nothing. You're smart and always find something for yourself. And I don't know anything. The car-service business is simple and is just for me. What do you think, Adam?"

"I agree, but I want ten big ones for my share now."

"Agreed. The buyer will come tomorrow."

The next day, Adam signed all the papers, got the money, and paid off his debt to Alex, hoping never to meet this person again.

Limousine Service

GOODBYE, ALEX, FOR GOOD. Adam got on the phone with Serge, who proposed doing business together in Manhattan. They joked that it would now be a limousine service from the former car-service owners. But Adam was mistaken. It became apparent that Serge was not suitable to be a partner either. At the first shareholders' meeting, he came without money, explaining that his father kept the money, whatever was there. Adam gave him another three days.

"If you don't bring the money, I'm going into business alone, but you, Serge, can remain as a driver if you want."

The mythical $5,000, of course, never was found, and it seemed that Serge was glad to stay as a simple driver. He brought in another chauffeur with a Cadillac limousine, a Hungarian guy named Janosh. Adam rented office space in Uptown Manhattan for $1,300 per month. He announced in the Russian newspaper positions for drivers with cars. He printed a promotional business card with a calendar on the other side, and every morning he carried them to nearby streets and distributed it on the windshields of parked cars.

The name of the new *"ZION, CAR-AND-LIMOUSINE"* service was written in red on the business card. The title proved unsuccessful, but it would become evident much later. For a while, very little business came in. Money melted away daily, and Adam cursed the day he climbed into the transportation business. It quickly became apparent that business was terrible. To keep it afloat, he needed to advertise, and advertising ate up the profit. So, the most significant part of that budget was spent on fliers and mailing lists. It proved to be a huge, time-consuming, complex process. All of Adam's energy went into the business, and gradually, it began to show results step by step. The customer lists and orders became more extensive, which was a pleasant surprise. The fleet had expanded, and there were two handsome limousines with bars, TVs, fridges, and other luxurious things. Such cars were called stretch limousines and were popular, especially on certain holidays. Also, the team of drivers has grown, and it was nice when Adam hired the two drivers from Alex's car service.

They complained about the bad luck and competence of the new partners. There was almost no work, and people had scattered like rats off a sinking ship.

New business gradually grew, but Adam worked from morning until late at night. He missed his family and felt unhappy because he only saw Nadia at night. It was sad that the child would grow up without him. He had terrible thoughts that the well-being of his family was built on sand. The business ate up almost all the money earned. Advertising ate away the remaining crumbs. There was hardly time for anything, even sleep.

* * *

Capital of Immigrants

Adam thought with horror of how to carve out half a day to bring his wife and child to the other end of town to Dr. Bass and Dr. Beer. One of the drivers told him about a children's doctor in the Brighton Beach area in Brooklyn. Adam called there and made an appointment for Nadia. The time came to visit a pediatrician for a regular checkup and another vaccination for Nadia. They heard Nadia's strange, unusual cough at night and were anxious.

"The good thing is that we go to the doctor tomorrow," Adam murmured, trying to take a little nap.

The doctor was a plump, middle-aged solid woman from Ukraine. She inspected Nadia, listened to her lungs, and concluded, "Well, she has a few coughs; it's okay. All children cough. It's time to get vaccinated. We'll do it now."

"Doctor, should we do it today? Maybe we can wait until the cough passes?"

"Parents, you don't understand. Immunizations should be done on time."

She prepared the syringe, opened Nadia's tiny hand, and pricked her. The child burst out weeping and choked from coughing.

"Oh, what a softy. Tomorrow everything will pass."

Adam and Nata discussed the new doctor on the way home, and then Adam raced to work. All day, he worried, with a bad feeling from the visit to the doctor. Nata phoned in tears late in the evening and said Nadia had worsened.

"She is so hot, and she cries with coughs."

"I must call this new doctor and ask what to do. We may have to go to the hospital."

He did so, but the doctor only snorted, "Oh, right away, go to the hospital! Young man, if all children were taken to hospitals, there would no free places. Small children often get sick. Stop having a tantrum. In two or three days, everything will go away."

Adam didn't believe his ears. He had left Russia precisely because of the unkindness and cruelty of people there.

This awful, disgusting doctor, eager to make ten dollars, vaccinated Nadia, and made the child sick, told me that all children cough. Now I must hear the same crap? How could someone do such things when a tiny, innocent baby suffered?

Adam cursed himself for his stupidity and could not understand—where was his head when he had decided to save a couple of hours and not go to the well-known doctors Bass and Beer?

He immediately dialed the number to the doctor's office and got Dr. Bass on the line. Adam explained the situation.

"Take the child to the hospital in Manhattan. Record the address. Tell them that your daughter is a patient in our clinic. I'll come there soon."

Adam closed the business and raced home, angry at himself and fearing for Nadia. She was sick. Nata and Nadia cried bitterly, first from the horror and second from the pain. Adam barely restrained himself from crying. This little creature was suffering through no fault of her own. He had allowed it to happen.

The nurse said a blood test from the vein was necessary for analysis at the hospital. Adam rolled up Nadia's sleeve. Her tiny hand was of the same thickness as his two fingers. He couldn't look at the needle going into the vein. A strict nurse in a white uniform came, and Nadia started screaming and coughing. Nata was close to hysterics; Adam was shaking. The nurse firmly took Nadia and went into the neighboring room. From there, they heard a harsh child's cry and the angry voice of the nurse. Adam and Nata embraced and wept bitterly. Finally, the nurse returned the child, and Adam grabbed her and instinctively held her to himself, unaware she was still alive.

Another nurse came and screamed at him.

"Let the baby go. The mother will stay with the child in the hospital, and you go home. Come in the morning. You understand?"

Adam, delirious, drove home, and all he could do was pray. His words were a prayer to God for help.

Lord, if someone has to be punished, punish me. I'm the one to blame for this. This tiny, delicate creature is not to blame.

The whole night was one big nightmare. Early in the morning, he rushes to the hospital. Nata and the baby seemed frightened and exhausted but were not crying.

"Dr. Bass stayed here for a very long time. Nadia had a little bit of water in her lungs. They wanted to pierce it and pump out the water, but Dr. Bass did not allow it. He said that he would observe her again today."

"God bless this man!" Adam didn't even notice that he constantly mentioned the name of the Lord, but he wasn't religious at all.

"Go to work. I'll call you and keep you up to date on everything." Nata sighed with relief. She called late in the afternoon. Adam's heart stopped beating, ready to throw everything down and rush to the hospital. But Nata reported good news.

"Nadia got better. They'll hold us a day more, just in case, and you can pick us up the next day. Dr. Bass said the child should not have been vaccinated in such a condition. And he even said we should come to him in three days for review."

"Nata, I swear to you, we will go only to him and Dr. Beer while Nadia grows. That filth made our child sick. I'll be dragging her to the courts. For those ten bucks, she'll cry bloody tears."

* * *

Adam started looking for a lawyer to take a case for a deliberate medical mistake. He dialed the law office number and presented the whole story, but in response, he heard, "If your daughter had died, then we could take that case of this."

"Better if you die, idiot!" yelled Adam in response, and he threw the phone.

Maybe finding this witch and cracking a brick on her head be easier. And then, who will feed my family while I'm in prison?

He smiled bitterly. Many evil thoughts were harvested and fermented in Adam's head, but he understood that this was nonsense and thirsted for revenge.

That rat cannot be punished by law, and I only hope for God's judgment.

Nadia was quickly recovering. She had stopped coughing and was already playing with her dolls.

On the appointed day, they went to Dr. Bass. Nadia immediately cried when he came to the room wearing a white coat. He went away and returned without the coat.

"Nadia, you see now? I have no coat. Do you like me better now? Yes, I see; so much better. Come on, let's see what you got there. How do you feel?"

It was all great. Nadia was healthy. And all the fear was a thing of the past.

* * *

Winter came. There was less work, although Adam still spent a lot of money on advertising. He couldn't get a break because it was a vicious circle—advertising, business, advertising. If he didn't advertise, orders became fewer and fewer. Spending almost all profits on advertising was necessary to keep the company afloat. Zion Car and Limousine Service, on the whole, brought less revenue. Only the limousines made good money. Most of the time, the work was only for limousines. Christmas and New Year's always attract many tourists to town. New York was full of music, sound, decorations, enormous snowflakes, and other wonders. People carried bags with presents and rejoiced at the new Christmas season.

Adam closed the office on Christmas Day and took the family to the Manhattan ice-skating rink and home of the big tree at Rockefeller Center. It was a lot of fun. Nadia laughed and clapped her hands, and Adam and Nata decided to celebrate Nadia's birthday the same way, having a new tradition every year. The day spent with his family was very short, and Adam knew that life with family was more important than any business. Sometimes, he glanced at his drivers, freelancers with their limousines.

They were independent, working here and there, depending on where the work was. They wore a beeper on their belts, trendy pieces that had only now appeared on the market. There was no need to have drivers sit at the office, which saved a lot of time. When they got a new signal, they immediately called the manager.

It would be good to get one of these limousines and a beeper. When I get a call, I could make some good money. I could work for myself and no longer have the headache of business issues. I could be at home and play with my child.

And it happened; his dreams came true. One of the limousine drivers came to the office with an unknown man. When Adam looked at him, he thought at first that he had seen him somewhere. But then he realized that he was looking at his twin brother.

"Adam, imagine my reaction! I saw this guy in Queens and asked, 'Hey, why are you not in the office? What brings you here?' And he answered, 'In what office?' Can you imagine that? Well, I begged him to come with me. You guys are the same as two drops of water. You must be relatives. Surely, you have some common roots."

"Hello, Adam. I'm Seva. It turns out that your buddy is not exaggerating. There is a striking resemblance between us."

"Yes, Seva. I'm impressed too. I was told sometimes that I looked like the actor Jursky. But I never met anyone who looked like me. Where did you come from?"

"From Odessa. And you, as I understand, are from Saint Petersburg? I never heard of any relatives in Saint Petersburg, although maybe there were. Who knows? In life, anything can happen. It is entertaining that you, it turns out, also work in the car service. I've been in this business for a long time but in Queens rather than Manhattan. And I'm not an owner so far. I have a partner, and we want to organize a business with transport if possible."

"Listen, Seva, and it's possible for you. You do not even have to organize anything; buy my business. I'm thinking of doing something else."

"Are you serious, Adam? Or are you joking?"

"I'm serious. Even today, I'm ready to give it up for ten thousand bucks."

"Wow! Come on. I'll call my buddy. He'll come here, and we'll discuss it."

"Do it directly from my phone. Yes, do not be shy; come here behind the desk."

Adam left his place and went outside with the driver who had brought Seva.

"Well, bro, if the deal goes through, you get a bottle from me."

"Are you for real? You want to sell the business?" He was surprised. "And what are you going to do then?"

"Like you, I want to work as a freelancer. I'm tired of all the headaches here. Will you help me buy one of those limousines?"

"Of course! Not a problem. I'll help. I'll also introduce you to someone who will do a deal. What are friends for?"

* * *

Sometimes, a miracle occurs when someone badly wants something, and everything works like clockwork. The scope and business potential of Zion Car and Limousine service impressed

Seva and his partner. They chatted and agreed to all the conditions without hesitation. Soon, Zion Car and Limousine service changed hands, and Adam was released with $10,000.

Adam's friend kept his promise and introduced him to another person. As it turned out, he had become acquainted with Daniel, the owner of a limousine dealership called Gaines, which occupied a large area in the industrial zone of Brooklyn. It was the largest limousine dealership on the East Coast. They handled maintenance, sales, and limousine insurance. The company owner, Mr. Daniel Gaines, was exquisite and fit. He was a self-made wealthy businessman. He was a child brought to the United States from Poland and became as strong and intelligent as the many who wanted to be real Americans. That man had made himself rich. He explained to Adam the nuances he should know when buying a limousine for work. To that end, Adam became the proud owner of a used Cadillac limousine for $28,000, and a large portion of this amount went to the loan account. Gaines insured the car and put it on full service.

An hour later, Adam was leaving the Gaines garage, worrying about not fitting on the road when making wide turns. This car was not just chic. It was a supercar, a Cadillac, a Fleetwood model with a powerful eight-cylinder engine. The mechanic who checked it out opened the hood and explained, "It's better not to go elsewhere for repair. If you get a problem, come or call. We'll do it."

Adam looked under the hood and saw the massive mechanism of pipes and wires. He couldn't imagine repairing it himself and would not risk breaking anything. These were the insides of the car, and they resembled a spacecraft.

Capital of Immigrants

Adam realized his new acquisition would barely fit in the allocated garage space at home. If this car were a little longer, he would have to look for a new parking lot, but it fits just enough to close the gate. At dinner, he and Nata talked about that limo. Adam was building new business plans. After dinner, when it got dark, and New York had its evening lights on, Adam started the motor and tried out the new family car. Nata and especially Nadia had fun. She rejoiced and clapped her hands in delight at the beauty. Adam lowered the glass divider from the driver's seat to the salon, which was the happiness, joy, and fun his family had. When they went on the highway, Nadia fell asleep, resting with the Cadillac's quiet rumbling engine and smooth movement. Adam, smiling, glanced in the mirror at Nata's shining face and thought he was adapting to America. Life had passed into a new phase. It was necessary to adjust to this new life phase and set aside money for Nadia's college. He meditated on all the thoughts that every family had when coming to this strange, unusual, and beautiful country of immigrants.

Ask Limousine

THE COMPANY WHERE ADAM WORKED as a driver was called Gotham. It was the same type of car service, but only with limousines of different luxury classes. Sedans, such as Cadillacs or Lincoln Town Cars, were most prestigious for business-class clients. A step above this was a limousine called Formal; it had an extended body, much longer than a sedan. The trip cost in this beautiful car was higher than in business-class cars. It was exceeded only by the level of the stretch limousine. Elegant interior, a bar with some glasses, ice baskets, alcohol, a VCR TV set, and a roof window. Adam registered his business under the name *"Ask Limousine."* All drivers were owners of cars and worked as freelancers with several companies, trying not to miss any opportunity to make extra bucks on luxury transportation. Each driver sought an opportunity to earn and intercept work before competitors. Like many others, Adam was obligated to pay the car installments; insurance wasn't cheap either, so everyone had to make substantial amounts monthly.

Most drivers gathered at the Gotham office at 10 a.m. They all wore beepers on their belts. They worked with two or three companies simultaneously, and orders could come from them anytime. A guy named Frank managed Gotham's business. He treated the drivers smoothly and without preference. When a new call came from a client, he repeated this to everyone, and the first driver who responded received the order.

On the first day, Adam received a job at 10 a.m.

"You have a customer on Park Avenue; take him downtown. Understood?"

"Of course! Thank you, Frank."

The pickup was located on the East Side of Manhattan. This residential part of New York was between Fifty-Ninth and Ninety-Sixth Streets. People who lived there were called "old money," the caste of the wealthy population and the aristocracy established long ago.

The same streets on the western part of the city were located on the West Side, and the people there belonged to the "new money" category. The vast Central Park divided those two parts of the city. Closer to the park, the avenues were more prestigious.

Park Avenue was well-groomed and respectable; it was the reputable area of the East Side of New York City.

There were many fashionable and large buildings with no offices or stores. The buildings had large driveways and mandatory liveried doormen, which confirmed the status of the inhabitants of these houses.

Adam pulled up to one of these mansions. The doorman inquired for whom the car had come, and a young lady in a business suit appeared with a briefcase in five minutes. The doorman led the lady into the car helpfully but with dignity. He opened the door and wished her a good day.

"Worth Street, please, and quickly. I'm already late." Now Adam realized that he had a problem. *Where is this bloody Worth Street? How do I get there? Okay, for a start, I must go to the East Side Highway and move toward the Brooklyn Bridge, where I can get off to the downtown area. If I'm lucky, there will be a sign to this Worth Street.*

But the sign wasn't on this cursed street. Adam panicked. He stopped the car and ran to a hot dog seller pushing a cart on the street. He had no idea where Worth Street was. Adam returned behind the wheel and continued moving in a stream of cars. He got the feeling that the client was becoming nervous.

She moved from side to side and said, "Sir, I am a lawyer, late to the hearing. Could you go faster? Do you know the way?"

"Yes, ma'am." It was Adam's only answer.

Then he saw a policeman. He was rescued. It turned out that the street was just the second right turn, and there was the damn Worth Street. The passenger jumped out of the limousine and vanished into the crowd. Adam felt like a complete fool. He would be fired if the client complained about him to the company. He needed to buy a map of Manhattan immediately and ride around the whole downtown area to learn it. It was so different from the central city. He did so, and the lawyer, thank God, didn't complain to the management of Gotham.

Adam soon became accustomed to the new workplace and thought about additional earnings.

Luxury car and limo services flourished in New York. All work was done by arrangement.

Capital of Immigrants

Picking up passengers on the street was forbidden. Private cars in Russia picked up passengers on the streets as a matter of course, but it was prohibited in New York.

Only yellow taxis with special licenses could pick up street passengers. This license was called a medallion and had to be attached to the yellow hood of the taxicabs. Picking up passengers without a license was punishable by revoking a driver's license and substantial fines. But despite such stringent rules, some drivers were always willing to make extra bucks. Many available cars were on the street sometimes and during certain weather conditions. There were not enough taxicabs in Manhattan during rush hour and severe weather. Luckily, some drivers could work a few hours to earn decent money.

Adam did not want to take this risk. He knew he would probably get the first job if he entered Gotham's office slightly earlier than ten o'clock. He enjoyed friendly relations with Frank, who willingly helped Adam get orders.

"I appreciate the loyalty and desire to earn, unlike someone who works from breakfast until lunchtime," said Frank. He had friendly feelings for Adam and once told Adam some personal stories.

"Only you come to the office every day seriously wanting to work. I also take my job very seriously. Once, I dealt drugs and thought I didn't know how to escape it."

"You used drugs?" Adam was astonished.

"No, I was a dealer. I sold drugs in Chicago. My boss knows about it. I said, 'I'll stop!' And I did. The truth is that we have some who indulge in the grass, but it's America. You have to watch what you do."

Adam saw how some drivers sometimes rolled cigarettes with marijuana. He was even offered it to try, but he firmly decided it was not for him. Adam would drink vodka or wine—yes, please—if he weren't behind the wheel. As for this other nonsense, he was not interested. There were some changes at Gotham. Competitors had some new things, such as radios, and the stream of Gotham customers became thinner. Therefore, the owner bought radio communication, and all drivers hooked radios into their cars. The apparatuses for connection were cumbersome and awkward but very modern and trendy.

The company could significantly save time searching for available drivers. It was a chance to restore the client base. Adam received one of the first radios and now didn't need to sit in the office; he had more opportunities to look for clients in the city.

One evening, Adam was driving on Forty-Third Street. The flow of cars barely crawled for an evident reason: numerous theaters between Sixth Avenue and Broadway. The shows started and ended at about the same time, and at this late hour, when performances ended, the theatrical public filled up all sidewalks and roadways. Many looked for taxis or other transportation, and all the cars filled the roads. Adam pulled his limousine to the side, hunting for people who needed a ride. And then, at his window, a man uniformed as a doorman was tapping. Adam dropped the glass.

"Hello, man! Are you free? Take two ladies to the Waldorf-Astoria. The ride is twenty-five dollars. Five dollars is mine. Is that cool? Then come back. You'll get another ride."

He opened the limousine door, and two brisk old ladies jumped in.

"What a bit of luck, thanks to you! You saved us. It's just a nightmare on the roads. But the show was wonderful."

They started telling Adam about the show they had watched.

"We specifically came from Cincinnati for the sake of a Broadway show. Wow, the musical, you know, it's truly something extraordinary."

They crackled incessantly and persuaded Adam to attend the play at first. Before they left, they gave twenty-five dollars with their thanks and goodbye.

After passing the same congestion, Adam returned to Forty-Third Street. The doorman brought a new couple into the car, shook Adam's hand while deftly removing the five dollars from his palm, and winked.

"My name is Peter. Take that couple to the Plaza Hotel, and return. The cost of the trip is the same as the previous one."

"I'm glad to make your acquaintance, Peter. I'm Adam. I'll be back!"

He rolled onto Broadway, and the road traffic became a little lighter. Peter was waiting with another couple.

"Sir, uh, Mr. Driver! Can you give us tomorrow a tour of New York? Peter told us that we could talk to you about city tours. My wife and I are from Ohio and have never been here."

"My name is Adam, and I gladly will be your guide. Tomorrow morning at ten, I can come to your hotel. The cost of my services is thirty-five dollars an hour. If you are okay with it?"

"Oh yes, Adam. Of course. We're Mr. and Mrs. Johnson. Nice to meet you. We have our wedding anniversary—fifty-five years. We came here to celebrate our anniversary and spend some money. We did not spend money for a long time, did we, honey?"

"Yes, dear! Adam, our children are grown, and we have not gone anywhere long. So, we have the rights." They laughed.

"Absolutely! I'm sure of it. And here is the Plaza. Tomorrow morning I'll be here at 10 a.m."

After dropping off passengers, Adam went to Forty-Third Street. The Johnsons told him about Peter, the doorman from Sardi's restaurant. They enjoyed that restaurant very much. Adam parked the limousine and went inside the restaurant. Sardi's was a magnificent and expensive restaurant located in the heart of the theater district of New York. Traditionally after the performances, the Americans went to have dinner, and in Broadway's vicinity, there was no place better than Sardi's.

Adam understood that if he became friends with this Peter, he could count on good earnings. From here, he had already secured excellent work for tomorrow, and of course, the tour would not be limited to one hour. Work like this could last three or four hours, maybe even more.

After each drop-off, Adam crawled along in a big traffic jam, looking for Peter. Usually, Adam noticed Peter's uniform hat from afar. They promptly shook hands and moved the money from hand to hand; Adam received new passengers and eventually returned. The financial results of the evening pleasantly offset his mild fatigue.

At 10 a.m. the following day, Adam was already at the Plaza Hotel. There were crowds of people. The doorman barely managed to open the arriving vehicles' doors and give a hand to exiting passengers. For this service, he received a dollar from everyone. Adam was stunned by how many dollars the doorman got in ten or fifteen minutes. Finally, yesterday's passengers appeared, and the tour began.

The elderly couple was charming, and Adam sympathized with them and gladly served as their guide. He showed them Manhattan, driving along the East River. They visited Spanish Harlem. They went up by Amsterdam Avenue to go uptown on the West Side. Adam wanted to show them the view of Manhattan from the island's highest point. A member of the Rockefeller family had built a castle at that spot, and now it was a great museum of the Rockefeller Foundation. The Johnsons walked up to the museum, admiring the view of the beautiful surroundings. Adam thought about how pretty and pleasant the view from this castle was. In their admiration for New York, there was something heartfelt. And most importantly, it was evident that the two had happily lived together for over half a century. They still cared for and loved each other.

The Johnsons returned ecstatic.

"Adam, we so appreciate it. We had never even heard about it. It's a charming museum and a magical gallery. We will tell our friends about it and how wonderful our tour guide was. And we will surely recommend you. By the way, can you recommend a cozy place for lunch? It seems that we are already hungry."

Adam drove downhill along the Hudson River, and they admired the fascinating view. He took them to Tavern on the Green, located inside Central Park, cautioning that the restaurant was expensive but had superb cuisine. And after lunch, he escorted them to the hotel. They had already been very friendly.

They exchanged phone numbers and agreed that Adam would take them to the airport.

"So, dear Adam, you have been with us for six hours. It's $210, correct?"

"Oh, yes, Mr. Johnson."

"That is for you, Adam. Keep the change, and we'll see you tomorrow morning."

The next day Adam took them to JFK Airport. Their parting was warm, and when they said goodbye, Mr. Johnson stretched out a $100 bill.

"This is for your Christmas baby. Pamper your daughter and wife."

"It's very touching." Adam was confused by such kindness. "You are such a nice couple. Thank you very much! And again, happy anniversary."

Atlantic City

AT HOME, a significant surprise waited for him. Adam usually bought some treats for Nata from the Russian stores—Russian yogurt and smoked sausages. Sometimes they wanted a nostalgic feast.

Adam came home earlier than usual. Nata saw him and got worried.

"Why are you so early? Did something happen?"

"Do I have the right to spend the evening with my family? I'm afraid that you will forget me."

"Since you're here, look what we can do. Kitten, show Daddy how you can walk."

"Oh, my God! Here's a miracle! Come to Daddy, baby. So, so—op-pa!"

Adam picked up Nadia and squeezed and kissed her.

"Who will call me Dad? Say 'daddy.'"

"Dad," the child clearly said.

"Nata, have you heard? She said 'Dad'! *Nadyushka,* say 'Dad' again!"

"Why is that? I'm with her all day. I play with her and bathe her; her first word is 'dad.' Why not 'mom'? Who will say 'mama'? Well, try, baby! Mom! Mama!"

"Ma … ma."

"Adam, Adam! Did you hear? Mom! My favorite! The sweetest little cat!"

They couldn't stop kissing the laughing child. Adam exclaimed with pleasure, "So, we agreed. We will go to the best toy shop and buy this miracle child the best toys."

"Adam, are we able to afford it?" Nata grimaced.

"Yes, we can. Today is a special day. I took a wonderful older couple from Ohio on a trip around New York yesterday. We chatted, and I told them about you and Nadia. Believe it or not, they gave me a hundred bucks for the baby today at the airport. So, let's go for gifts."

* * *

Adam resurrected old ties. He called Gena; in the old days, he had introduced Adam to Alex. Gena and Alex were friends for a long time, but they parted ways. Adam arranged to meet with Gena's family, wife, and son.

Gena also wanted to meet with Adam for a long time. They had worked together in Russia and were friendly. That had been in that old life, but now Adam decided to restore this old friendship. Therefore, Gena, his wife, Ira, and their son, Max, were invited. As judged by Adam, Nata spent days sitting at home, and her social circle included only Nadia and two teddy bears. The feast turned out great, and even the usually shy Nata cheered up, rejoiced, and promised to cook something from her mom's recipes next time. These parties at each other's houses soon became a weekly tradition.

* * *

Adam worked practically every day. His duty was to deliver whatever Nata and Nadia needed. This way of life was typical for an American family. Adam hoped Nadia would not need to fight for her place under the sun when she grew up. He did not want her to struggle as he and Nata had as immigrants. Nadia's life should be easier and happier.

Working as a limousine driver wasn't what he had dreamed of, but it allowed him to make a living. Adam hoped that he could accumulate the start-up capital for their own business. Things were going well at Gotham, and his friendship with Peter, the doorman of Sardi's restaurant, developed to their mutual benefit. When Gotham had no orders, Adam went to Broadway to find Peter and usually made two to three trips per night.

However, he did not restrict his business dreams to restaurants and culinary things—everything Adam loved and experienced. He increasingly returned to franchising—maybe a fast-food restaurant or a café. The motivation for this was his lunch at Kentucky Fried Chicken.

Every time he watched the operation, he wondered how fast and efficiently they serviced customers. Orders were collected in the boxes incredibly fast. Adam wondered if he could run such a business by himself. To begin with, he couldn't afford to hire anyone, which seemed possible in this kind of business. Looking around, he saw what food people liked.

Everything was prepared: fried chicken, fries, mashed potatoes, and coleslaw. Adam sometimes bought a lunch box consisting of two pieces of chicken, a biscuit, and a choice of salad or mashed potatoes. Everything was delicious.

I must learn how to deep-fry chicken. People buy such food willingly because it is well known, but there is space for something new. It doesn't have to be a famous joint; it could be a small one-person store. Then I could find where to buy all this packaging and prepare it as the guys do at Kentucky Fried Chicken.

While driving people in his limousine, he always looked at the buildings with signs advertising "premises for lease."

It's got to be a desirable location, preferably a place already somewhat adapted for the restaurant business. I need gas, electricity, and a place that only needs minor cosmetic repairs.

Adam knew he could buy professional equipment for cafés and restaurants on Bowery Street. He could find everything for such a business: raw materials and product packaging. There was secondhand equipment, but it was in decent condition. There were cookers, ovens, refrigeration units, and secondhand kitchen equipment suitable for every need and budget. That was part of the problem. The cost of starting up a small business was more or less determined. As for now, all earned money was going toward payments for the limousine, apartment rent, and keeping the family afloat, which the Americans called the cost of living. The only source of income so far was the limousine. Adam had no suitable luxury of getting ill, having an accident, or damaging the car for any reason. The lack of a safety margin had become the most challenging ordeal. He should sit behind the wheel until the last moment and somehow balance on edge, change his status, and become a businessman. Anyway, he had to bring money home.

* * *

Capital of Immigrants

The following Christmas, Adam warned Frank at Gotham that he would work only until six in the evening. He was ready to go home to celebrate Nadia's birthday. And, as usual, there was a last-minute challenge: a trip to New Jersey worth more than $250. He could not refuse.

Firstly, it was an easy job and decent money. Secondly, Frank had requested it. He knew that all the limousines were busy on Christmas Eve. That was the hottest time for limousine services.

Adam called Nata and reported that he would be a little bit late. He drove on Fifth-Fourth Street and pulled up to the hotel where he was supposed to pick up the client. There was a deserted hall—only a bored receptionist behind the desk who said his passenger would be down in fifteen minutes.

Adam decided to warm up the car and got back in. He turned the ignition key, but nothing happened. No light bulb lit up. Nothing worked. The starter did not crank. No sounds. Adam tried to start the vehicle again, but the result was the same. The limousine was dead.

Adam panicked. What had happened? Was the battery dead? Or had it been stolen? Adam, trembling from overwhelming fear, lifted the hood. It looked as though everything was in place. The battery, belts, and other parts of the car looked normal. What was he supposed to do now? Call a repair shop? And who would take the customer to New Jersey?

Another limo braked next to him.

"Hey, buddy! What happened? Need help?"

"God must have sent you. Listen, if you are free, I have a job to take a passenger to New Jersey."

"Where exactly? And how much money? What's wrong with you?"

"I can't do it. The battery went dead or something else. Will you help?"

"Let's try. I have the cable here. Try to start it up. We'll see if this battery will start."

Together they tried to start the car. Adam turned the key and—oh, a miracle! Lights went on. Everything flashed on the dashboard. The flywheel reluctantly, slowly twirled, and nothing was more enjoyable than this rhythmical humming sound. To Adam, it seemed that it was still alive.

"Thank you, friend! The work is yours—$250 to New Jersey. And Merry Christmas to you, my savior. Tell the client that you are from Gotham Limousine."

Adam gladly gave the booking away and drove home. He had made the right decision. The car could seize up again, and he could be stuck in New Jersey. It would be suicide.

He hoped the battery would last the ride home, but according to Murphy's Law, the car froze in the middle of the street near Fifth Avenue. Behind him, there immediately formed a convoy of dissatisfied drivers. Scolding and insults ensued everywhere.

"Hey, you, limo! You're blocking the road!"

"Guys, I broke down. Please help move the vehicle out of the way, and then all of you can move."

Piles of snow were everywhere. Several men helped push the limousine to the side. It was possible to bypass it despite being barely out of the way. However, this did not reduce the drivers' anger. All kinds of mocking cries and derogatory jokes poured on his head.

With frozen hands, in the dark, Adam searched the glove compartment for the business card of the insurance company and repairman. He managed the task with luck, then clenched the card in his trembling fingers. Adam had the phone number and ran back to the recently left hotel. His teeth were chattering, and his hands turned blue when he entered the hall. The porter asked what was wrong and allowed him to make a call.

The telephone rang for a long time, and Adam despaired. But then a female voice on the other end of the phone asked if he needed help. He told his story.

"Where are you stuck?" asked the young lady. "You need a flatbed or a tow truck?"

"What? I do not know. What is the difference between a flatbed and a tow truck?"

"If the car can't move, it must be loaded onto a flatbed platform and taken in for repair. It can be hooked up to a tow truck if transported."

"Then I need a tow truck. I think maybe there is a problem with the battery. The car itself is intact but dead."

"Wait for our driver. Considering the snowfall and traffic jams, it will probably take about three hours."

Adam was horrified.

Three hours? There goes my Christmas with family. It's my daughter's birthday. And what do I say to Frank?

He called Nata with the story. He didn't expect her reply.

"Thank God nothing happened to you. And if it had happened on the highway? Even thinking of it is too scary."

"Everything is fine, but I don't know when I'll get home. Maybe not till early in the morning. Congratulate Nadia for me, and go to sleep."

* * *

Adam spent the next two-and-a-half hours in the hotel lobby. The staff already knew his story and had given him some tea. They would not send him out in the frost. But he had to return to the car and wait for the tow truck. Finally, it showed up in the heavy traffic going down Fifth Avenue. Adam realized that the driver would have to drive around the block to pick up his car, and he ran toward the hotel, hoping to catch the tow truck on the road. But the awkward tow truck moved around the block another hour. Adam tore his hair out, watching traffic, counting the minutes. Finally, the needed assistance arrived.

"You've broken down? Where is the car?"

"Near Fifth Avenue. I saw you when you were driving down."

"Why didn't you call me? I drove around here for more than an hour. Brother, why are you dressed like that? It's not the month of May. You're probably frozen to the bones."

"Frozen completely. Can you take me to my home? I'll pay."

"I'd happily do so, but with a limousine to tow across town, I can't."

"Okay, I'll catch a taxi."

"Hurry up and get home. Drink a glass of vodka. That's the right way to do it. I also want to go home. My wife curses all the holidays we must work. Come on; give me the keys, and catch a taxi. Good luck to you."

* * *

When Adam arrived home, Nata and Nadia were already asleep. Adam drank one full glass of vodka, quietly lay on the sofa, and dove into darkness. In the morning, he called Frank and told him about his misadventures. There was nothing to discuss regarding the car; it would take time to repair it. So, he dropped out for a few days and could spend time with his family. He was not required to give up everything and go somewhere. Adam could be on the couch, watching TV. He could play with his child all day and communicate with his wife.

It was genuine happiness—nothing else he wished to do.

On the third day, he went to the repair shop and saw his limousine parked far down the parking lot. Adam was furious and went to the boss.

"Why did you leave my car and not even take it in for repairs? I already haven't worked for three days!"

"Your car has been ready for a long time. The generator was replaced, and that's it. You can take away this beauty. Pay in the office; the cost was $550."

On the way back from the workshop, he thought about why he had engaged in this business. A lot of money ran through his hands. But the cost of living, insurance, and extreme situations swallow the entire income. The result of the challenging work and suffering was still the same. And there were also moral costs. Not all customers were similar to the couple from Ohio. Recently he'd had to work the whole night with drunken, rich loafers, clearly from wealthy families. They had been rude, unpleasant, and indifferent to everything except their pleasure. They wasted money left and right, driving around to clubs and pubs, and by four in the morning, they could barely speak. They drank and roared with laughter, screaming out of the window and yelling nasty things at the entire city. They spilled champagne inside the limo.

Adam waited for them in the limousine during the last stop at some bar. He felt a hard blow on the car and heard a terrible grinding sound from the front bumper. Adam jumped out of the car. He saw another car race away at breakneck speed, without lights and a ripped-off corner of the back bumper. It seemed that the car had flown and was now going to burst.

The drinkers returned from the bar. They did not even notice the accident and continued screaming and having fun.

"Man, we all have skated enough. We'll drive to our hotel."

One of them gave his credit card to Adam, not even asking for the sum, and signed for the charges.

I worked ten hours with these drunken bastards. I earned three hundred fifty dollars, and another bastard hit me, scratched the car, and damaged the bumper. The repair will cost about two thousand five hundred dollars. Insurance does not cover bumpers. Always something is not covered. So, what do I have? Everything is wrong. Why do I need such work? But there is no other yet.

Adam gripped the steering wheel and continued to move forward.

* * *

He had one of those rare days off with his family that spring. They had gotten out on the beach and set up a picnic. Then Adam received a call from Gotham. It was an exclusive offer—pick up four West-Side passengers and take them to Atlantic City. Adam and Nata weren't upset; it was an hourly fee of thirty-five dollars for a trip no fewer than nine hours. Both knew that money talked.

Capital of Immigrants

Atlantic City was an alternative to Las Vegas for nearby East Coast residents. Those who liked to gamble found many casinos, and the largest, at the time, was the Trump Plaza. Adam delivered his customers there. There were boxing competitions, beauty pageants, and magnificent shows.

"We are here. You have four free hours. If you decide to stay longer, it's another thirty-five dollars per hour. I'll wait for you here."

The passengers rushed into the casino, and Adam went there to see how people spent their time. He wasn't going to play.

I don't want to spend any of my money on this. I want to kill time; that's it.

The casino was huge and divided into several zones. Everywhere stood one-armed bandit slot machines. They take quarters, fifty-cent coins, and dollar coins. The players were primarily older people. Some played with two or three machines. Sometimes some of the machines started ringing and flashing colored lights. People who got lucky were happy winners, and others threw coins in even faster, hoping to win.

Then there were the blackjack, poker, and roulette tables. Adam walked past crowds of people playing at all the tables. Some were playing craps. Someone rolled dice; others made some bets. Adam tried to understand the complex system of this game but couldn't.

He had four hours to kill here—and maybe even more. There was nothing to do at that time but gamble. Adam searched his pockets and found a few quarters while passing by one of the slot machines. He dropped a few into the slot machine for good luck. It was silly to visit the casino and not spend at least a dollar!

He yanked the handle. Automat went crazy; the screen flashed numbers and signs. Then the shapes exploded; the lights flashed, and loud, noisy sounds rang. Adam was scared at first; it looked like he had broken something. The man beside him said, "You're lucky today! Congrats!"

Adam realized that he had won. The machine rang and shone so much that one could see and hear it from either end of the vast hall. Confused about his tremendous luck, he just sat and waited, but no one came. He did not understand what was going to happen next. People congratulated him on his good luck, but the machine did not give any coins; it simply lived its brightest life. It lasted a few minutes, and Adam felt stupid.

What must I do? Sit and wait? Search for an employee who explains where to pick up the winnings. Could nobody see or hear that I needed help? Such noise and ringing! Could I maybe play at the next machine while waiting? But it's impossible to sit there, doing nothing.

Finally, an employee in a uniform appeared; turning the key, she silenced the machine.

"Congrats! You won $250. Here is your money. Thank you for choosing our casino!"

She slipped him some dollar bills and then retired. Adam looked at the money and did not know what surprised him more: that $1 had turned into $250 in ten seconds or why there was so much hustle and bustle about this amount. With the sounds and lighting effects, he would have thought he had won a million.

Okay, what now? Go to sleep in the car? How do I sleep now? The free money is burning a hole in my pocket. As the

Capital of Immigrants

Americans say, "Easy come, easy go." Maybe I should kill some time by playing. And if I lose, I still have lost nothing; it wasn't my money.

He had always dreamed of trying poker. He chose the desired video poker machine, and in an hour and a half, he had won another $200. Adam recounted his chips and could not believe his luck. Rather than stopping, he decided to bet big.

Excitement took over his head. But the most terrible thing started when he moved from poker to roulette. The chips went quickly, and he began to bet on his own money. Start with the first hundred and then the second, third, and fourth. In addition to that money, he also had cash from his customers. His mind told him not to touch it; however, gambling fever had taken hold. His temptation to win back the money outweighed the arguments in his brain. Adam tried to regain the lost winnings and bet on everything. He moved from table to table and stopped only when the money ran out. And then he woke up. The pain of the gambling hangover was hard.

Oh, what have I done? What a moron! How could I lose the family money? To hell with what I won—but the family budget? I went on a mission! Idiot. It's time to stop these senseless fares, limousines, and casinos. Damn them to hell! Tomorrow I should start looking for a spot for the business.

* * *

The passengers returned in exactly four hours. Adam raised the partition separating the back seat from the driver's seat. He silently watched the rain on the road, strengthened in his resolve to quit this work as a driver and do what he had always wanted: start his own business in New York.

That experience with the casino had told him things to do, and it seemed he had turned the right path. He was no longer a green immigrant, trapped by a need for survival and leading a desperate struggle for continued existence. There will be more ups and downs. But he only had two choices: to remain as he was or to break out and overcome.

END OF VOLUME I